COLOURING INDIA

Mindful Colouring with Festive Rangoli Patterns

EDITED BY
BHAVI MEHTA

hachette INDIA

First published in 2016 by Hachette India
(Registered name: Hachette Book Publishing India Pvt. Ltd)
An Hachette UK company
www.hachetteindia.com

SRD

ILLUSTRATION CREDITS
TITLE PAGE: padmajagraphic/Istockphoto.com; INTRO PAGE: kumarworks/Istockphoto.com; INTERIOR: p. 1 © KatikaM/Istockphoto.com; p. 2 © KatikaM/Istockphoto.com; p. 3 © INDECcraft/Istockphoto.com; p. 4 © KatikaM/Istockphoto.com; p. 5 © Matorinni/Istockphoto.com; p. 6 © KatikaM/Istockphoto.com; p. 7 © jsabirova/Shutterstock.com; p. 8 © HappyJack29/Istockphoto.com; p. 9 © HappyJack29/Istockphoto.com; p. 10 © IrinaKrivoruchko/Shutterstock.com; p. 11 © Zinaida Zaiko/Shutterstock.com; p. 12 © Zinaida Zaiko/Shutterstock.com; p. 13 © krishnasomya/Shutterstock.com; p. 14-15 © AnnaGarmatiy/Istockphoto.com; p. 16 © Art and Fashion/Shutterstock.com p17 © AnnaGarmatiy/Istockphoto.com; p. 18 © Bhavi Mehta; p. 19 © Zinaida Zaiko/Shutterstock.com; p. 20 © Naticka/Shutterstock.com; p. 21 © Mashot/Istockphoto.com; p. 22 © Vera Volodkina/Alamy Stock Vector; p. 24 © Snezh/Shutterstock.com; p. 25 © KatikaM/Istockphoto.com; p. 26 © Snezh/Shutterstock.com; p. 27-29 © KatikaM/Istockphoto.com; p. 30 © Snezh/Shutterstock.com; p. 31 © KatikaM/Istockphoto.com; p. 32 © Anikakodydkova/Shutterstock.com; p. 33 © Olesia Agudova/Shutterstock.com; p. 34 © Snezh/Shutterstock.com; p. 35 © AnnaGarmatiy/Istockphoto.com; p. 36 © Snezh/Shutterstock.com; p. 37 © Julia Snegireva/Istockphoto.com; p. 38 © Snezh/Shutterstock.com; p. 39 © Lolla Lenn/Shutterstock.com; p. 40 © Ira Mukti/Shutterstock.com; p. 41 © zzayko/Istockphoto.com; p. 42 © KatikaM/Istockphoto.com; p. 43-46 © Snezh/Shutterstock.com; p. 47 © Shpak Anton/Shutterstock.com; p. 48-49 © Devil08/Shutterstock.com; p. 50 © Solyannikova/Shutterstock.com; p. 51 © Snezh/Shutterstock.com; p. 52 © KatikaM/Istockphoto.com; p. 53 © Snezh/Shutterstock.com; p. 54 © pixelliebe/Istockphoto.com; p. 55 © Snezh/Shutterstock.com; p. 56-57 © totallypic/Shutterstock.com; p. 58 © KatikaM/Istockphoto.com; p. 59 © Snezh/Shutterstock.com

Cover and book design by Bhavi Mehta

ISBN 978-93-5195-159-9

Hachette Book Publishing India Pvt. Ltd
4th & 5th Floors, Corporate Centre,
Plot No. 94, Sector 44, Gurgaon - 122003, India

Printed and bound in India by
Manipal Technologies Limited, Manipal

MIX
Paper from responsible sources
FSC™ C043100

Rangolis are an integral part of all festivals and celebrations in India and also grace the entrance to homes as auspicious symbols.

These beautifully decorative patterns are referred to by a variety of names in different Indian states and among different communities. In the southern state of Andhra Pradesh they are known as a *muggu*, and in Kerala and Tamil Nadu they are called *kolam*. *Chowkpurna* in Chhattisgarh and Madhya Pradesh, *mandana* in Rajasthan, *aripana* in Bihar, *alpana* in Bengal, *rangavalli* in Karnataka and Maharashtra, *alikhthap* in the hills of Kumaon, *ossa* in Odisha, *saathiya* in Gujarat and *sonarakshana-sanjhi* in Uttar Pradesh –their patterns remain as varied as their names.

Traditionally painted using coloured rice, coloured sand, coloured flour and even flower petals, every rangoli marks a joyful celebration, with patterns ranging from simple geometric designs to delicate lotus flowers, dainty fish, elaborate paisleys, sparkling diyas and intricate peacocks. And here they are on the pages of this book – waiting for you to bring them to life!

Get inspired and colour away!

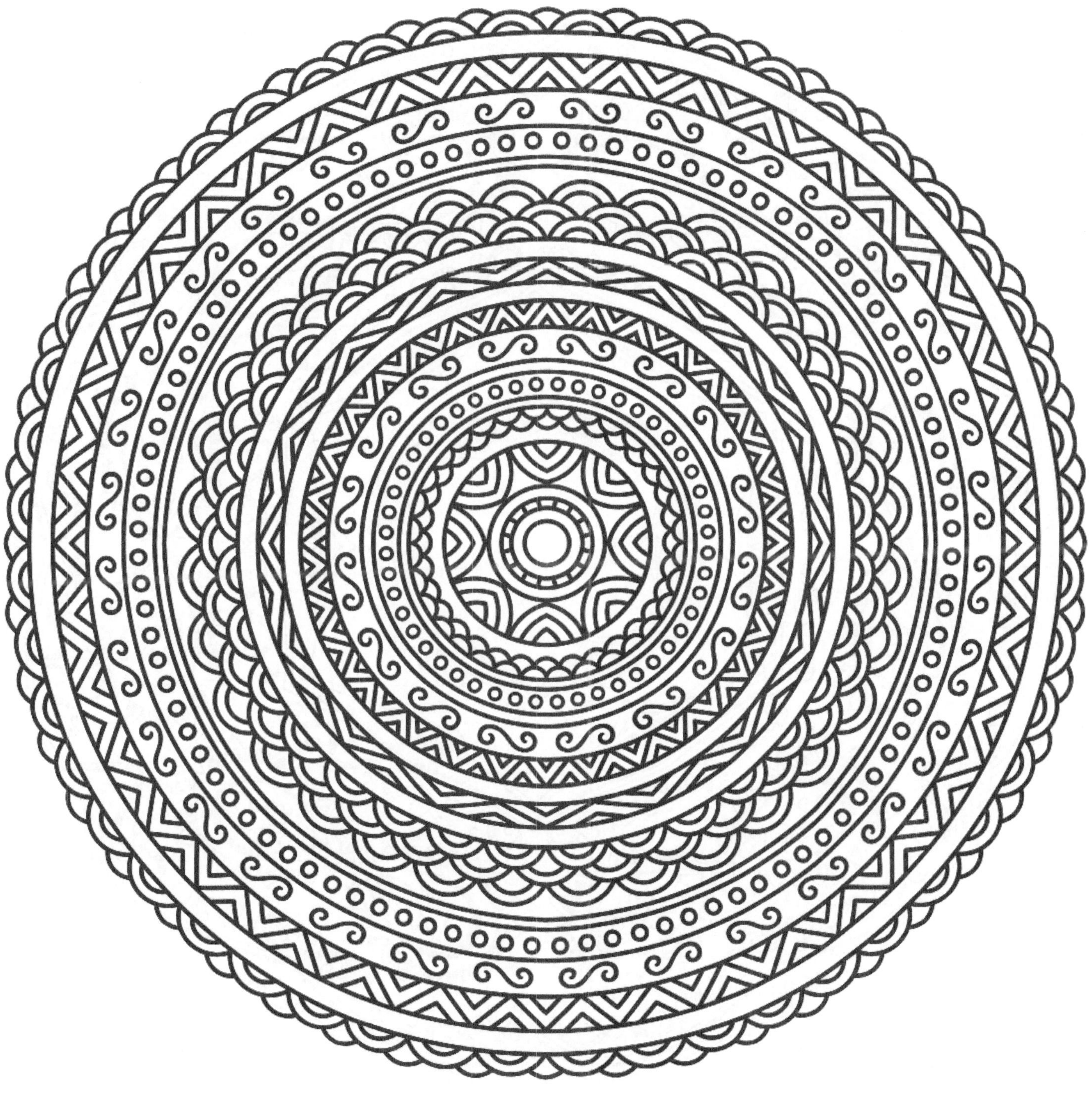

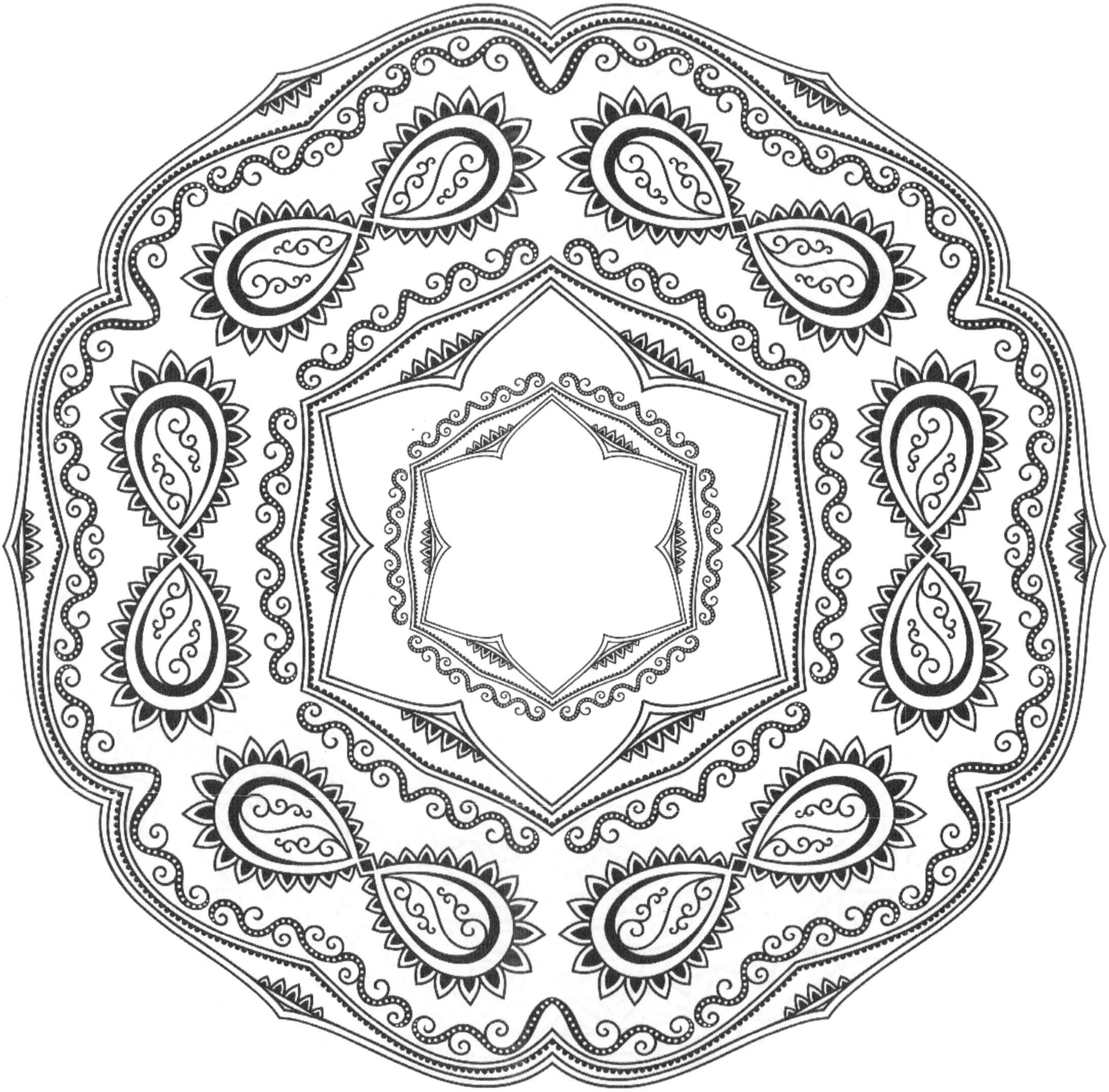

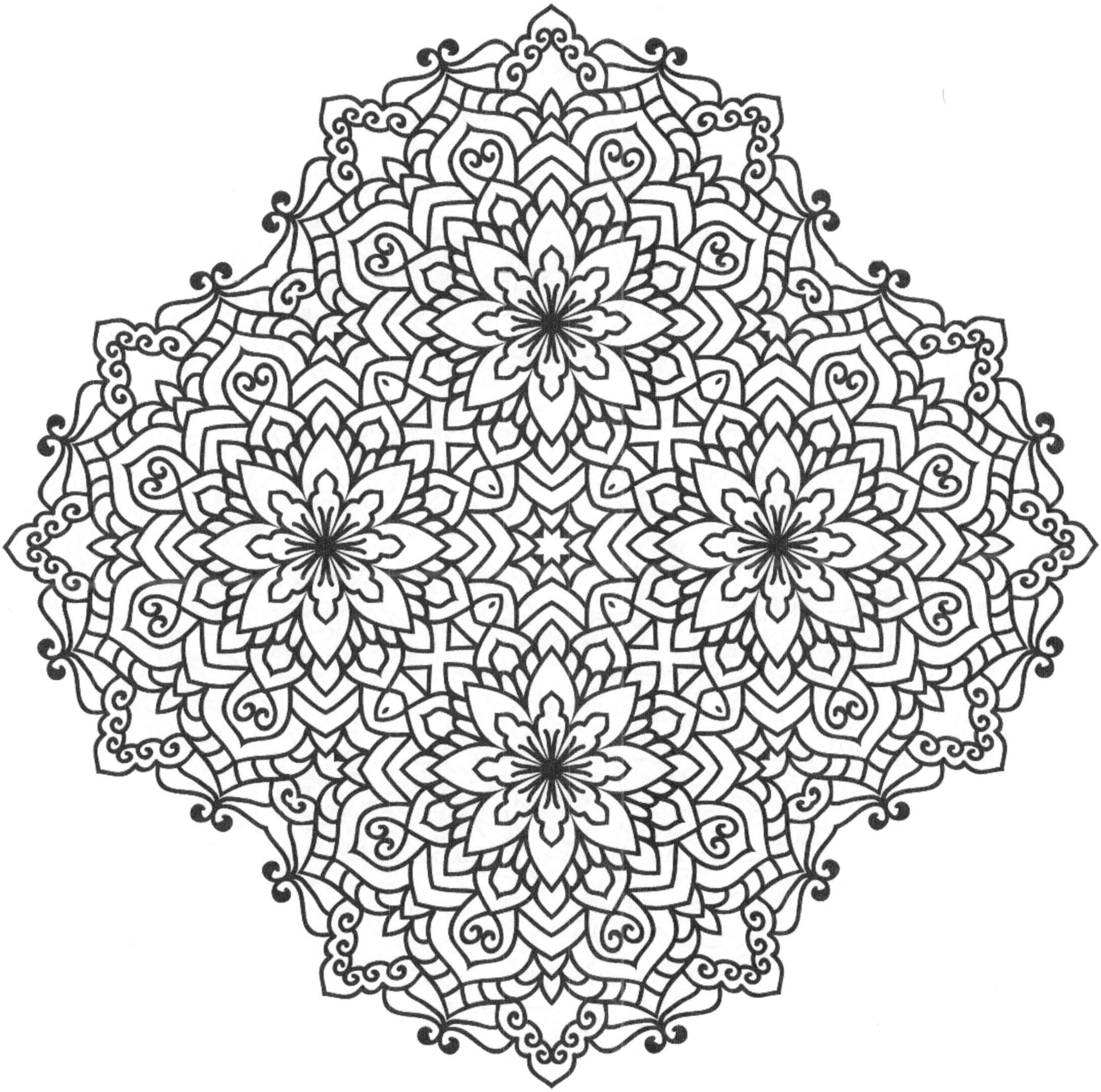

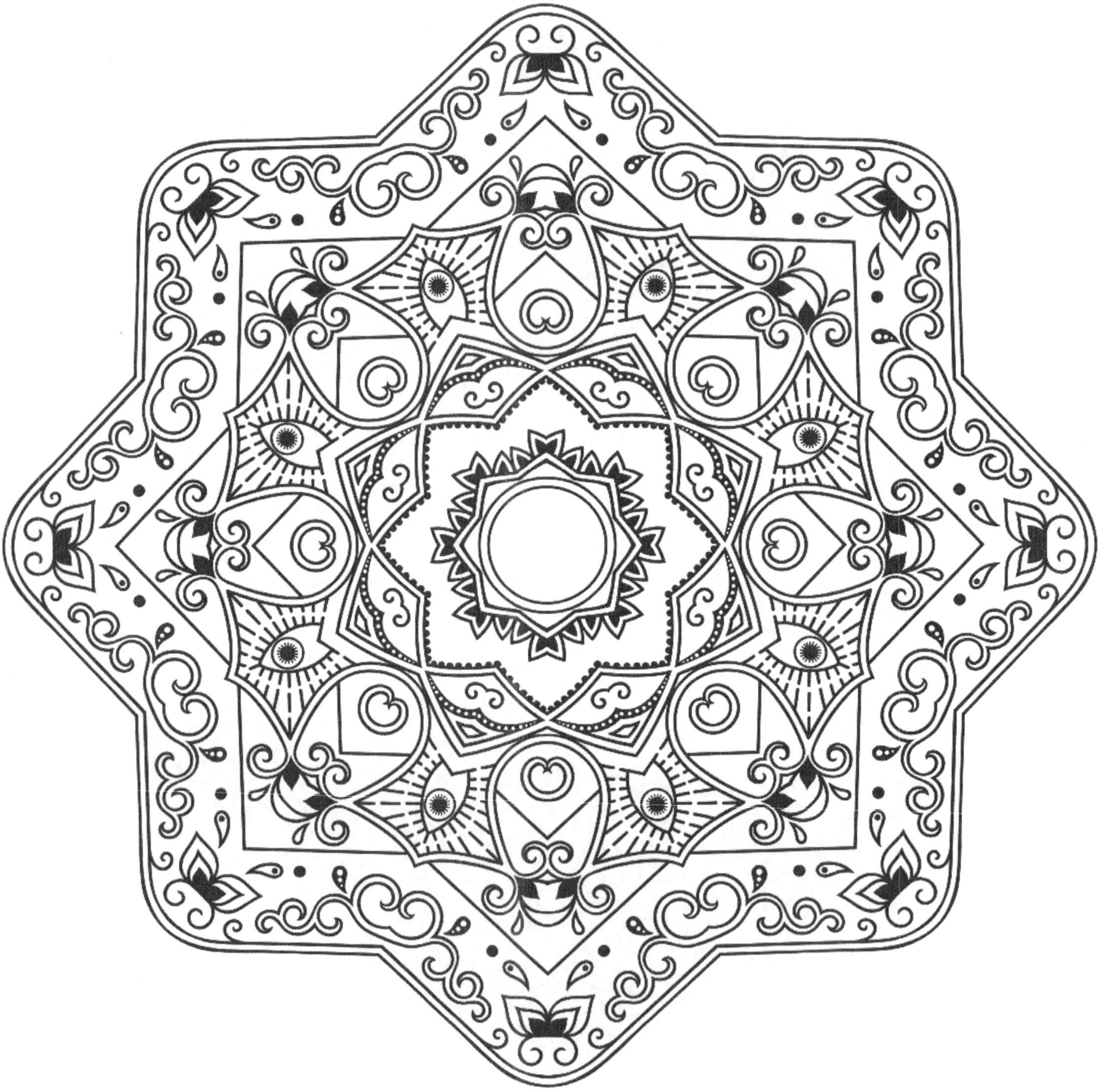

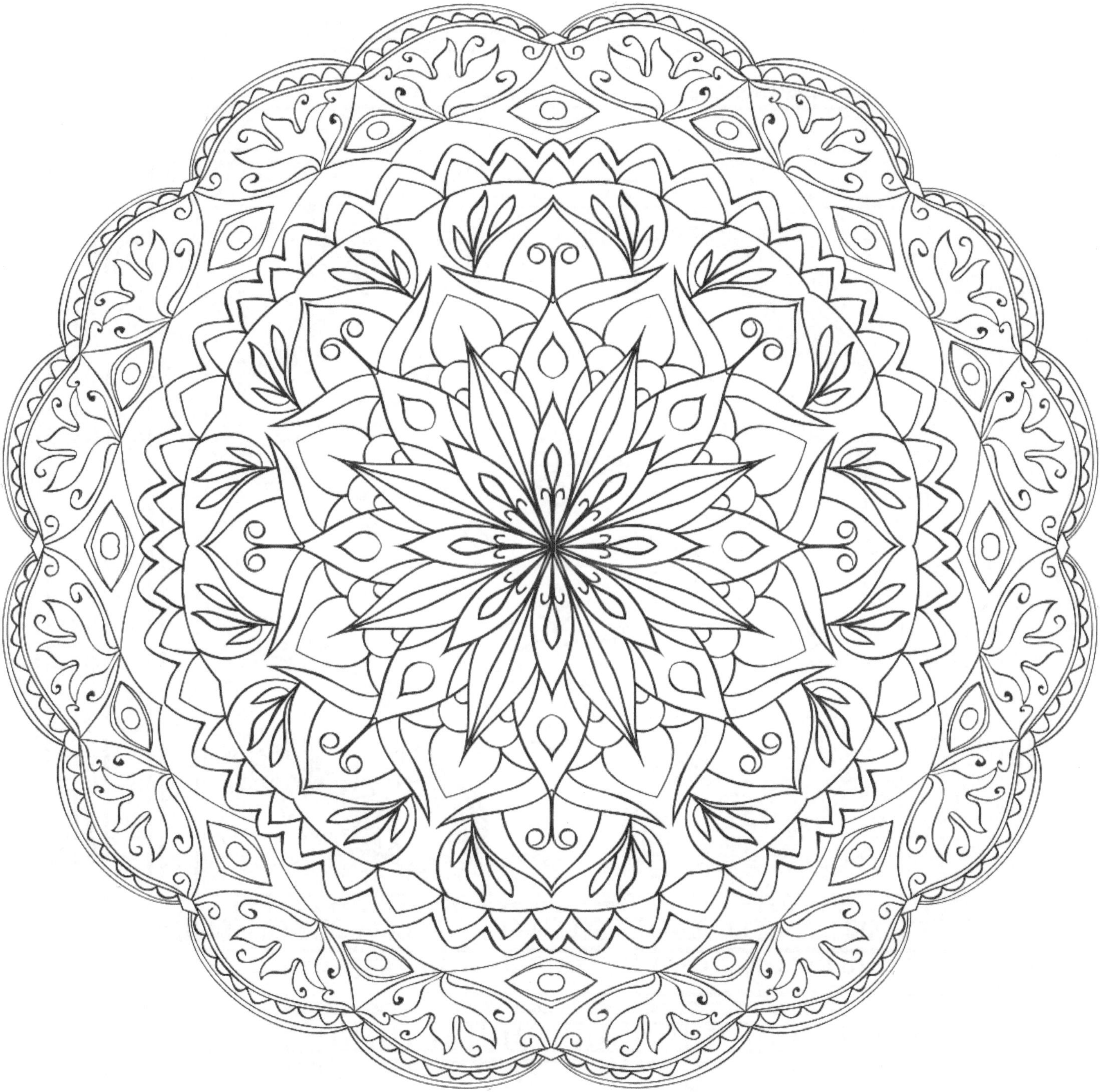

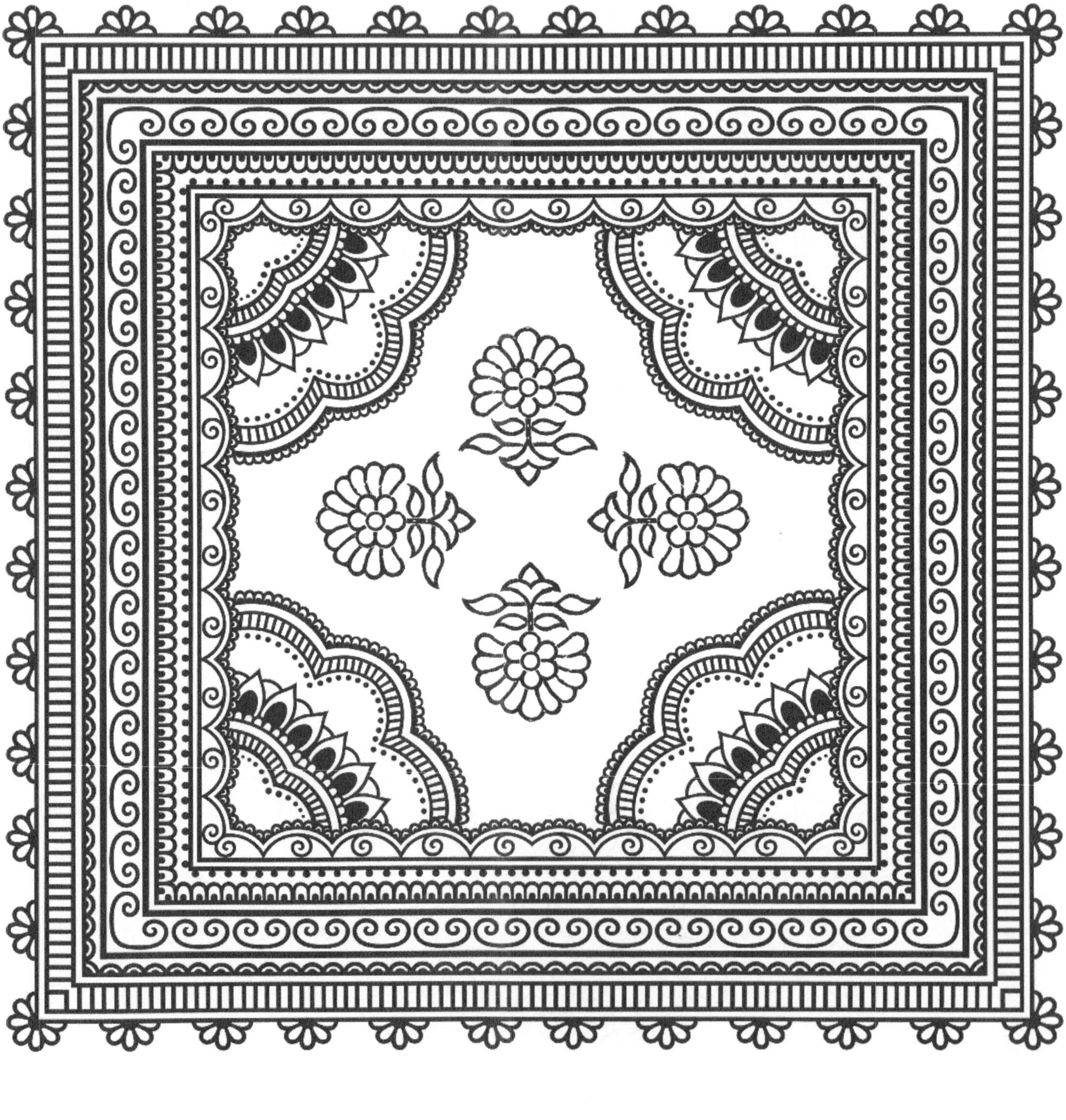

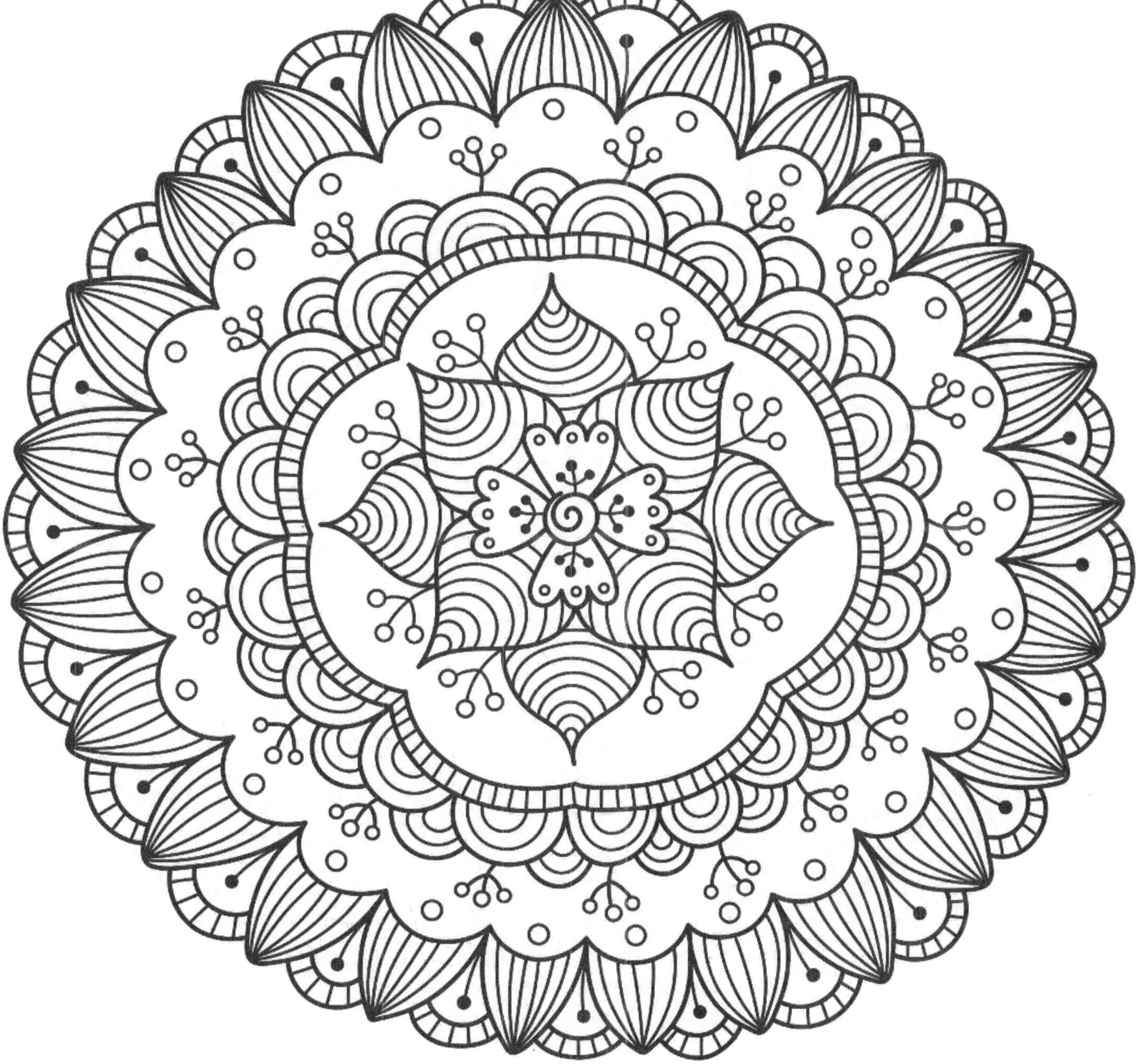

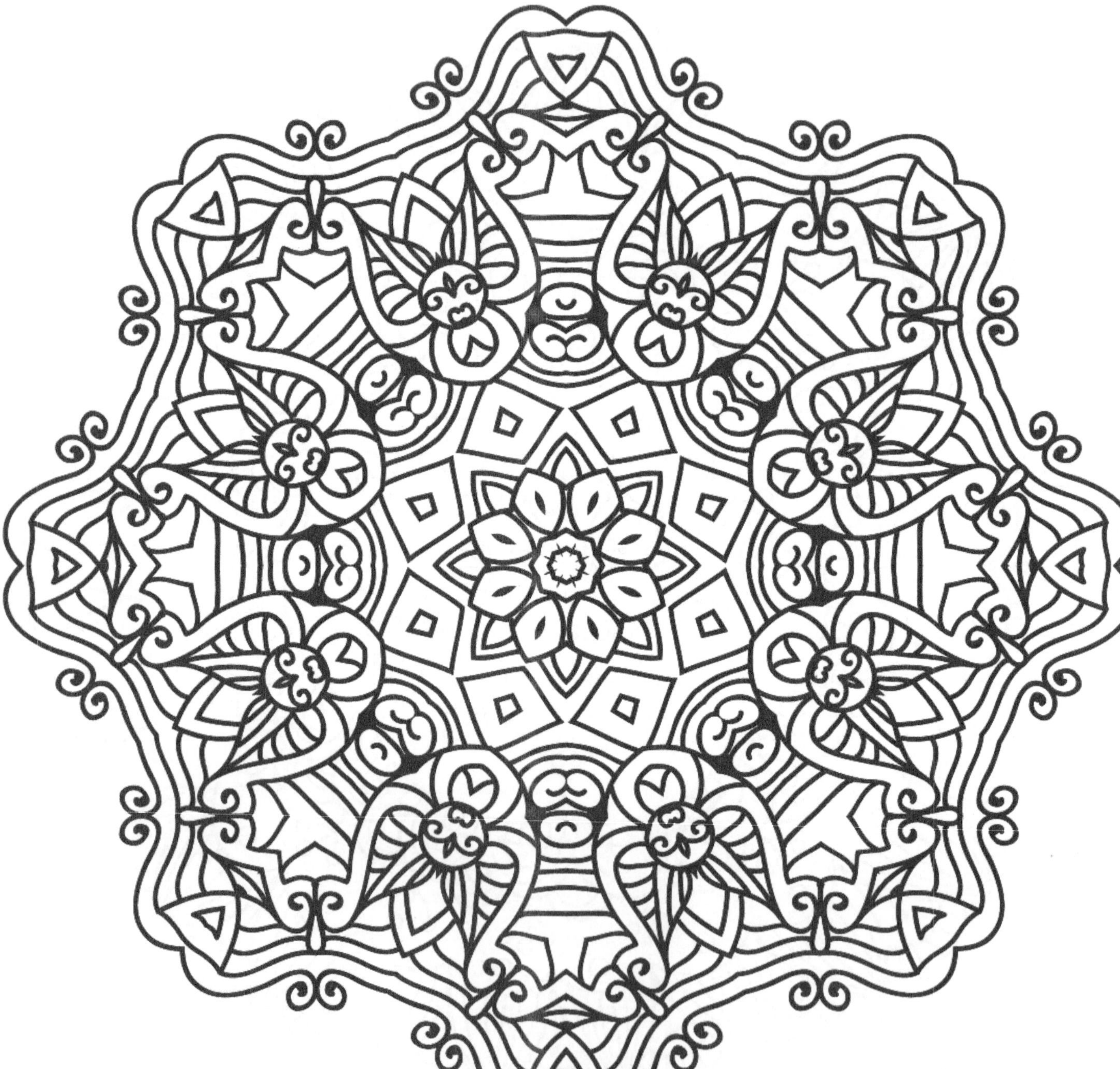

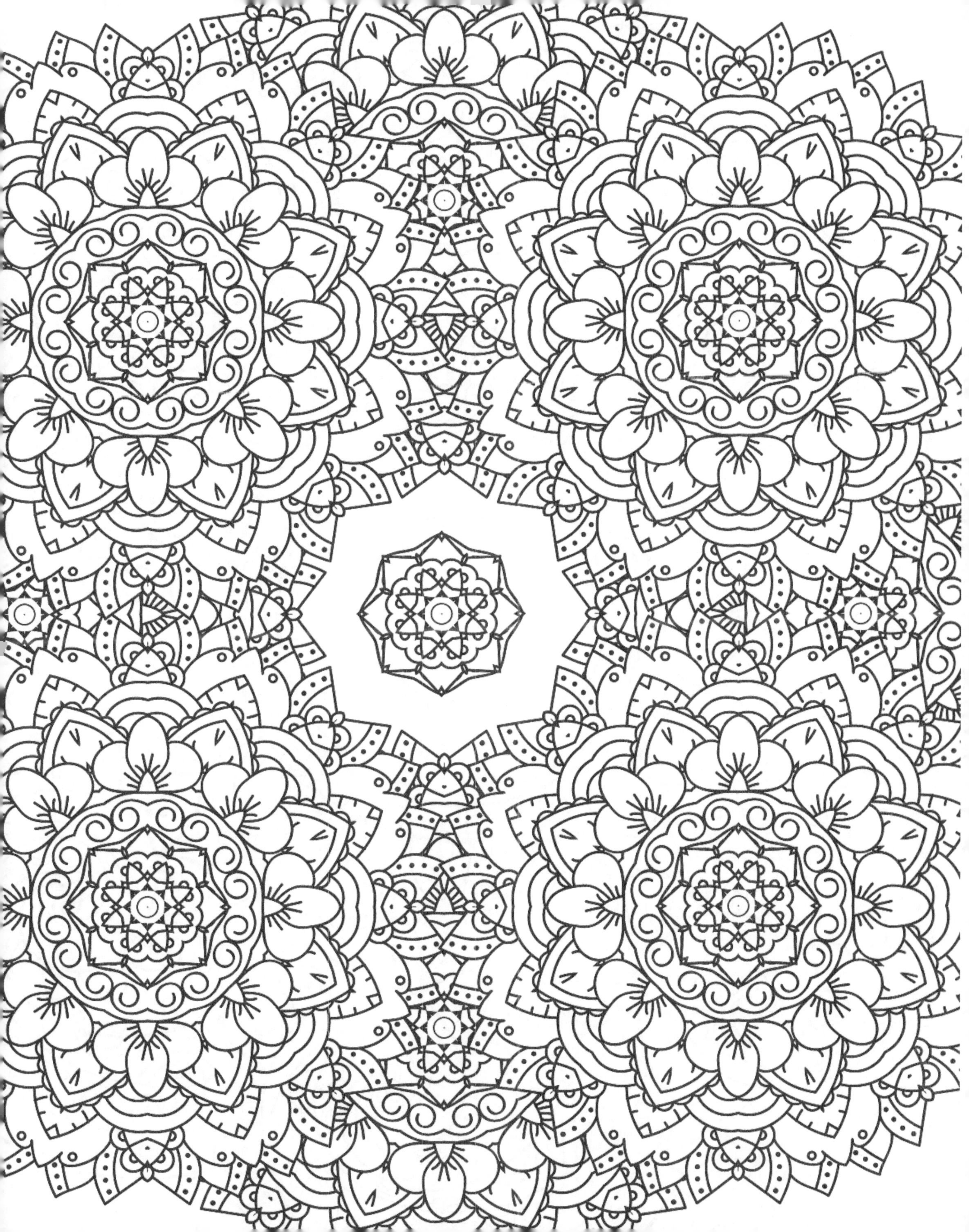

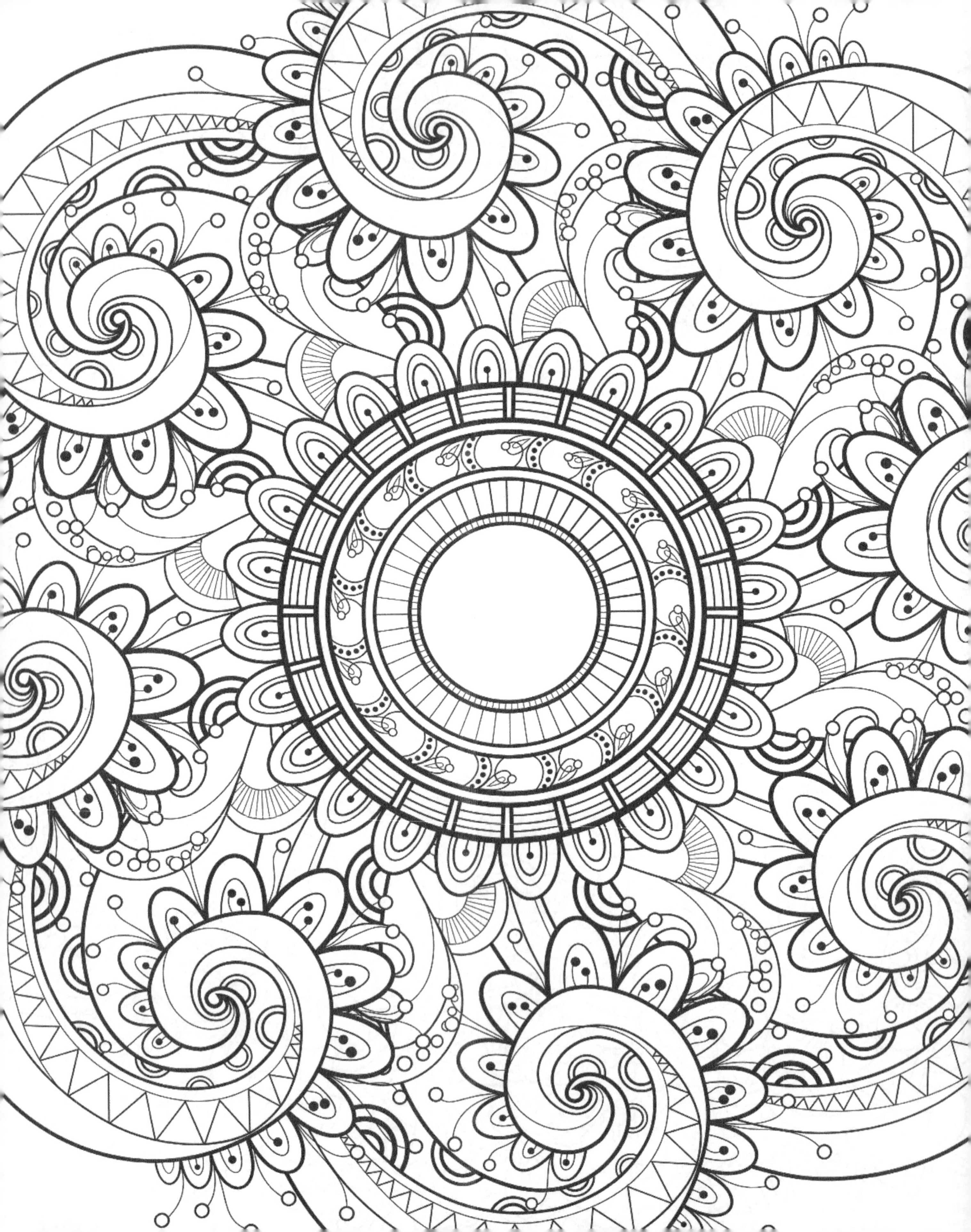

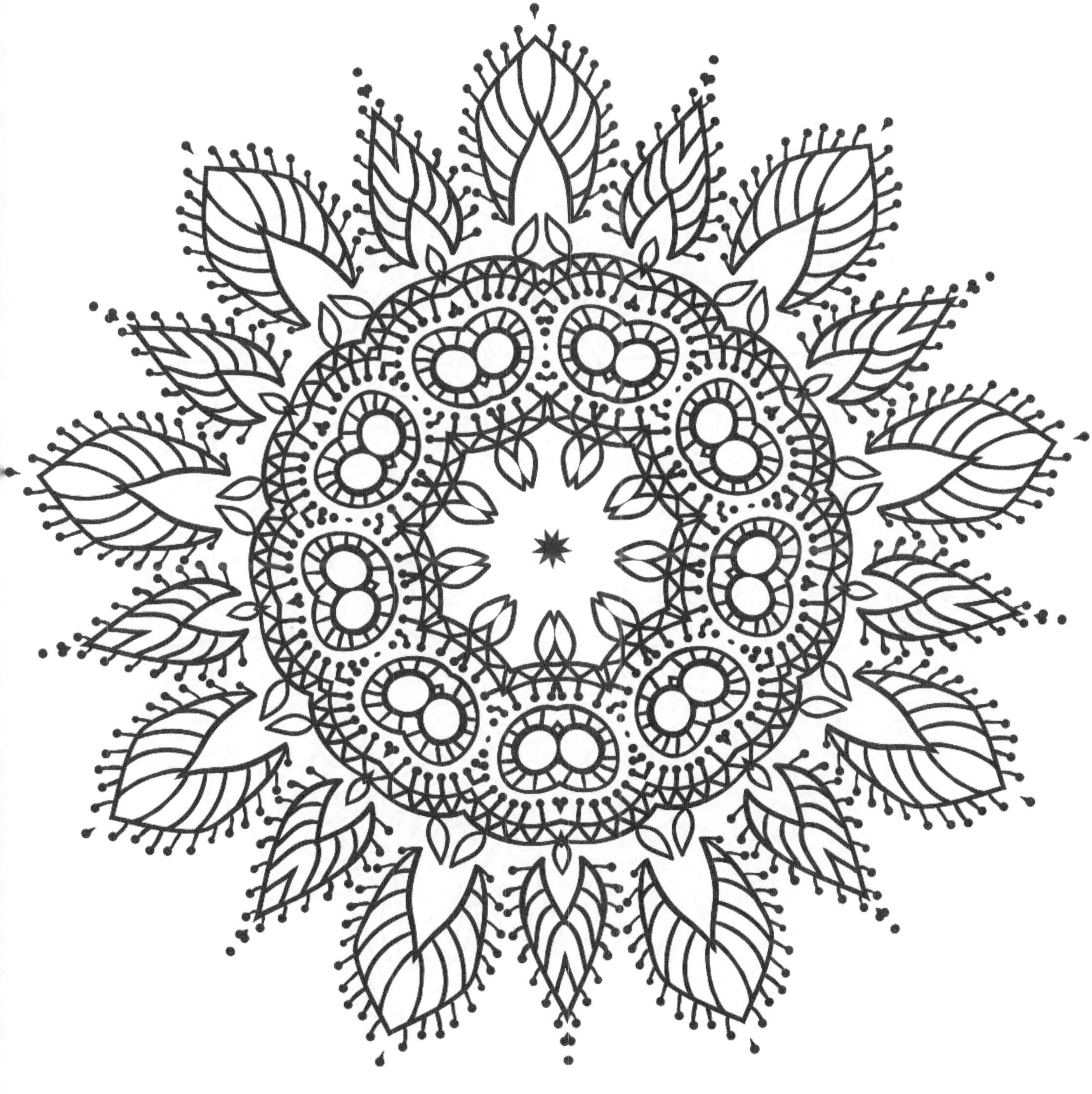

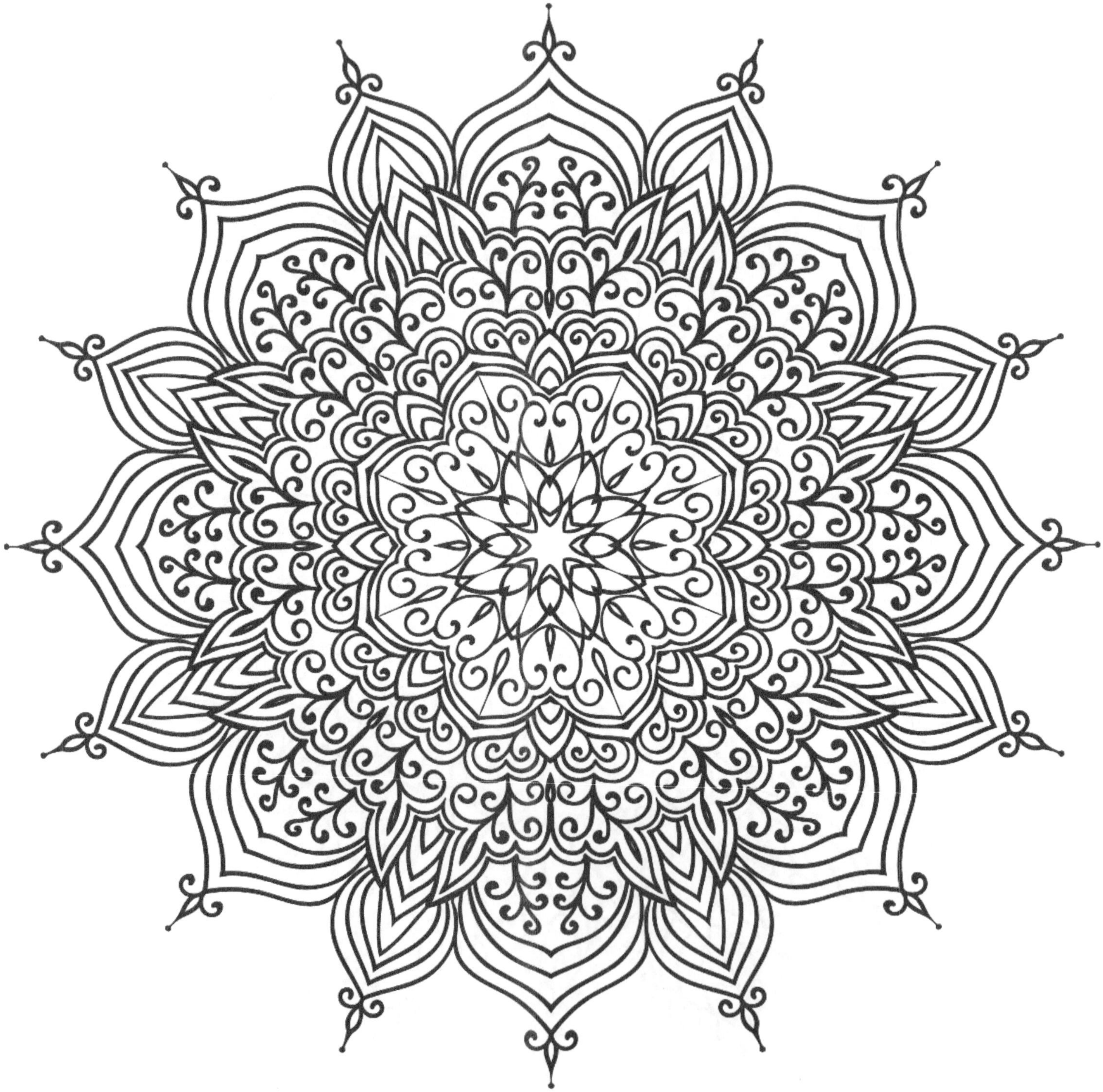

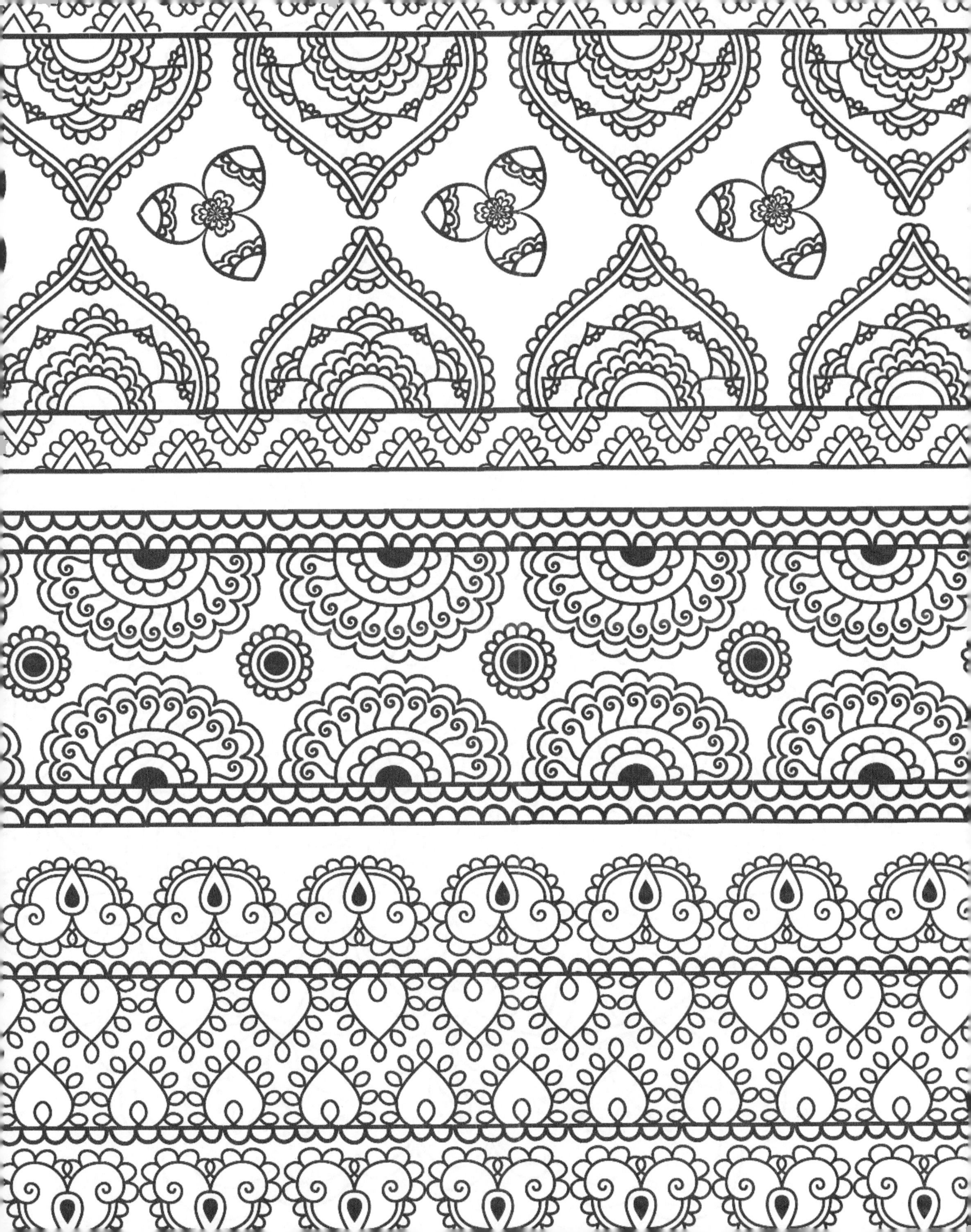

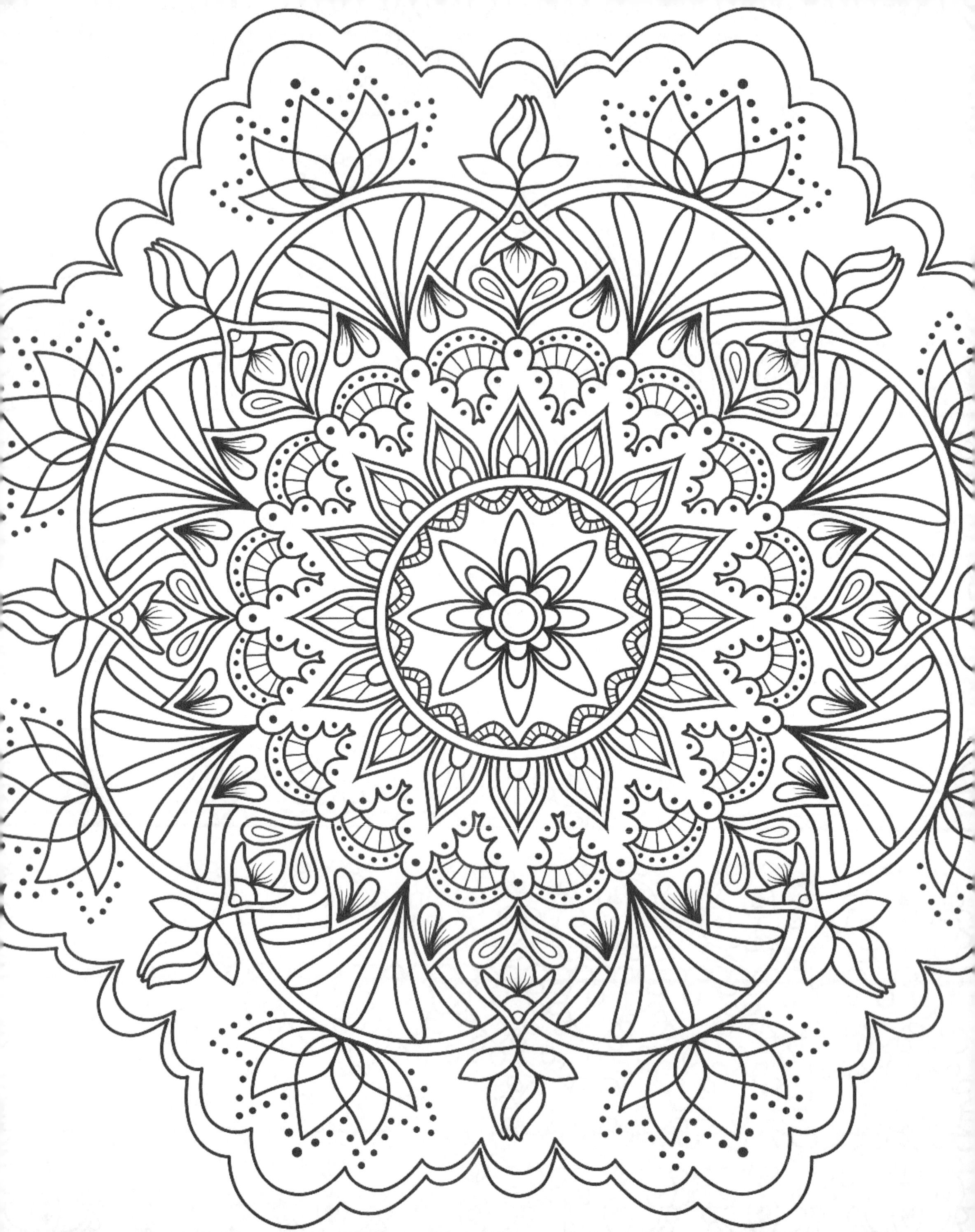

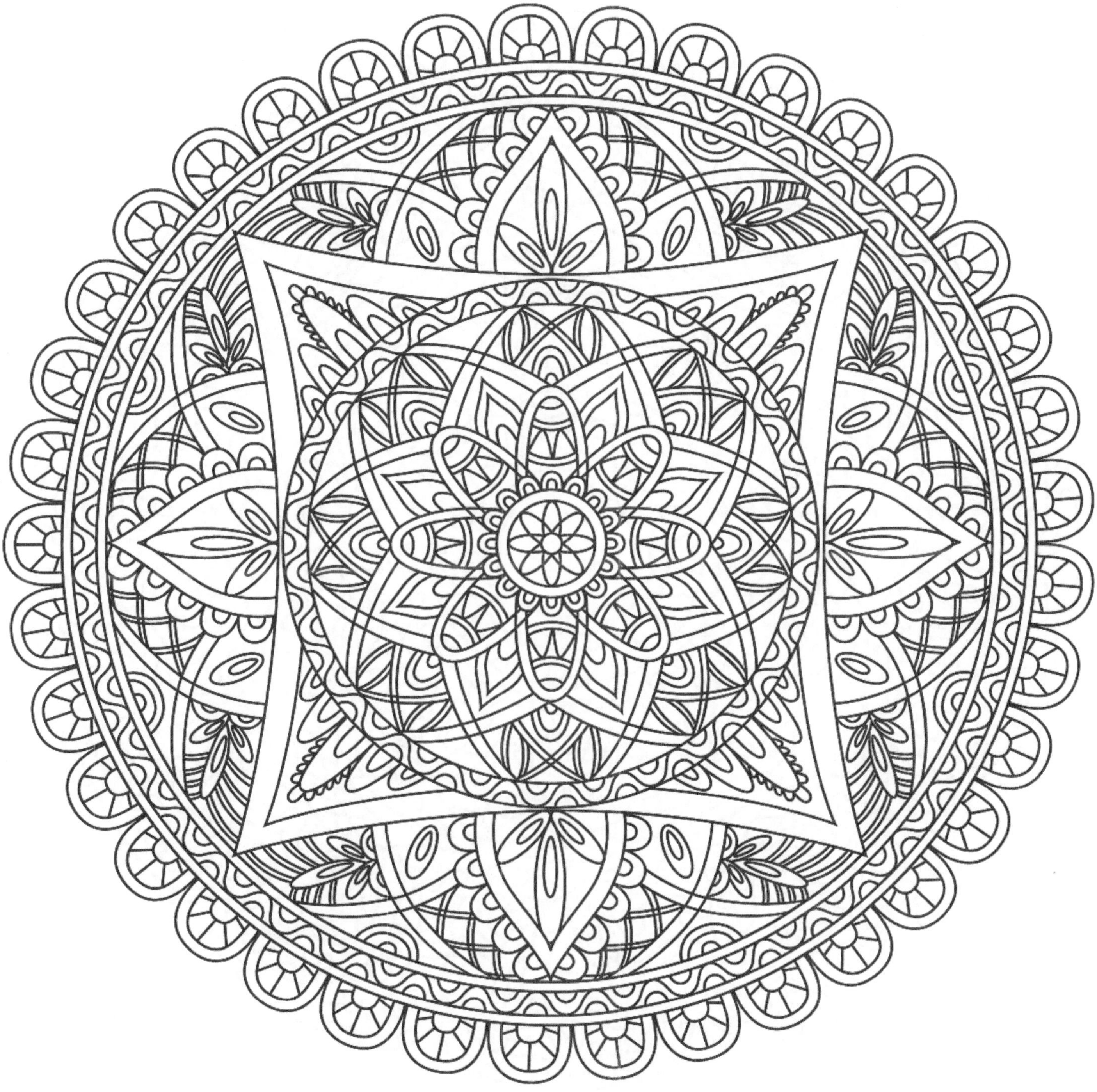

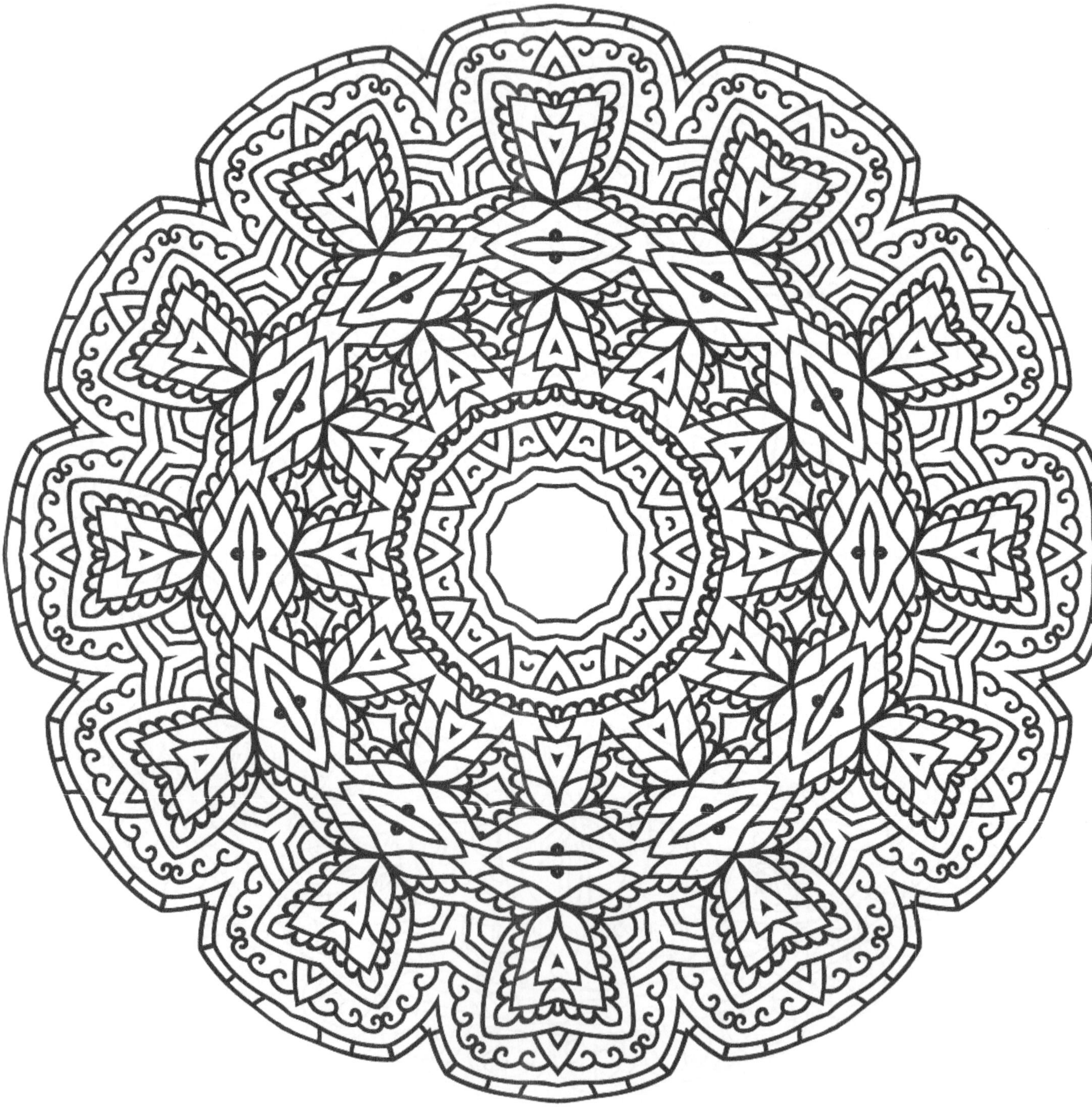

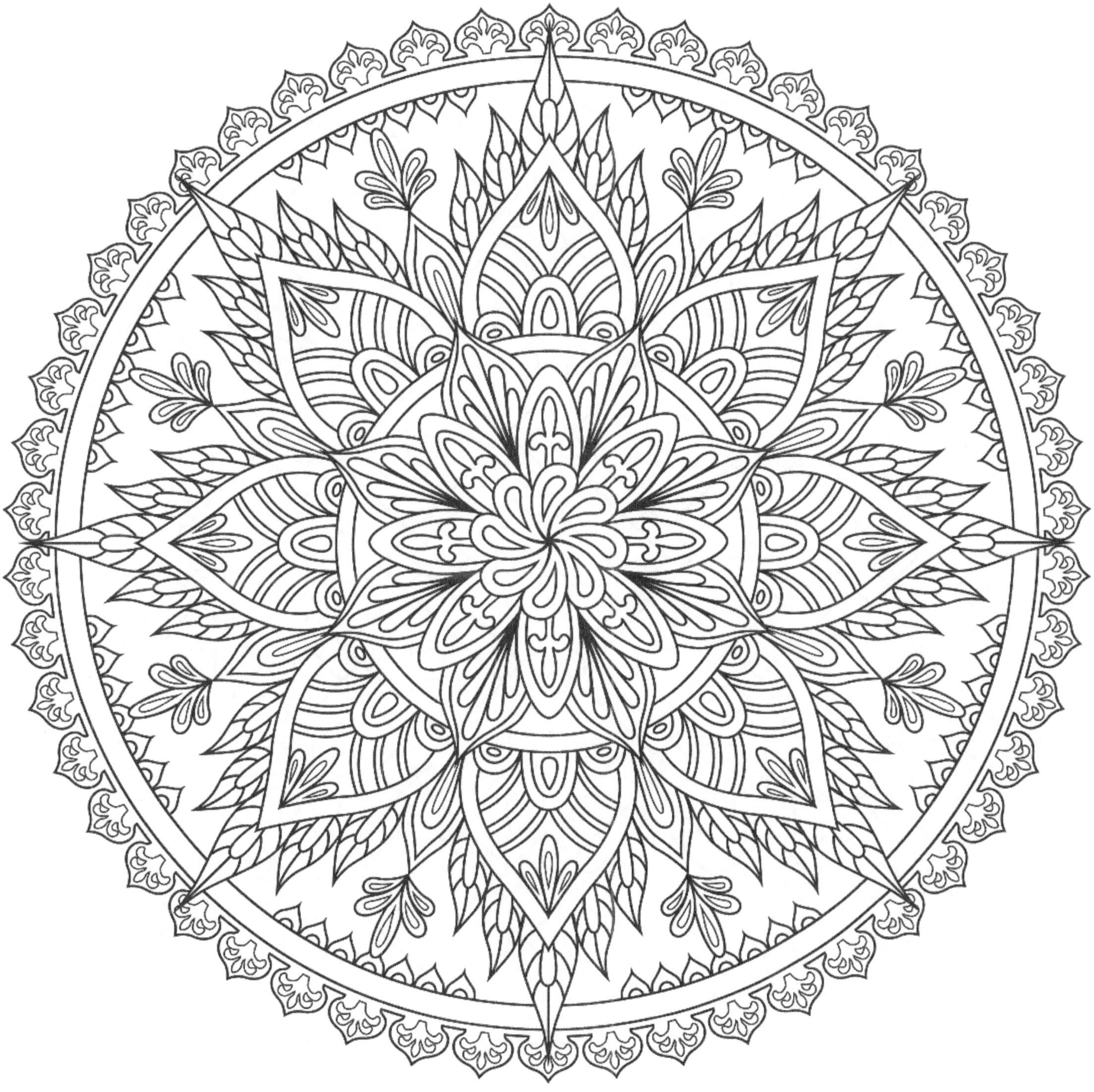

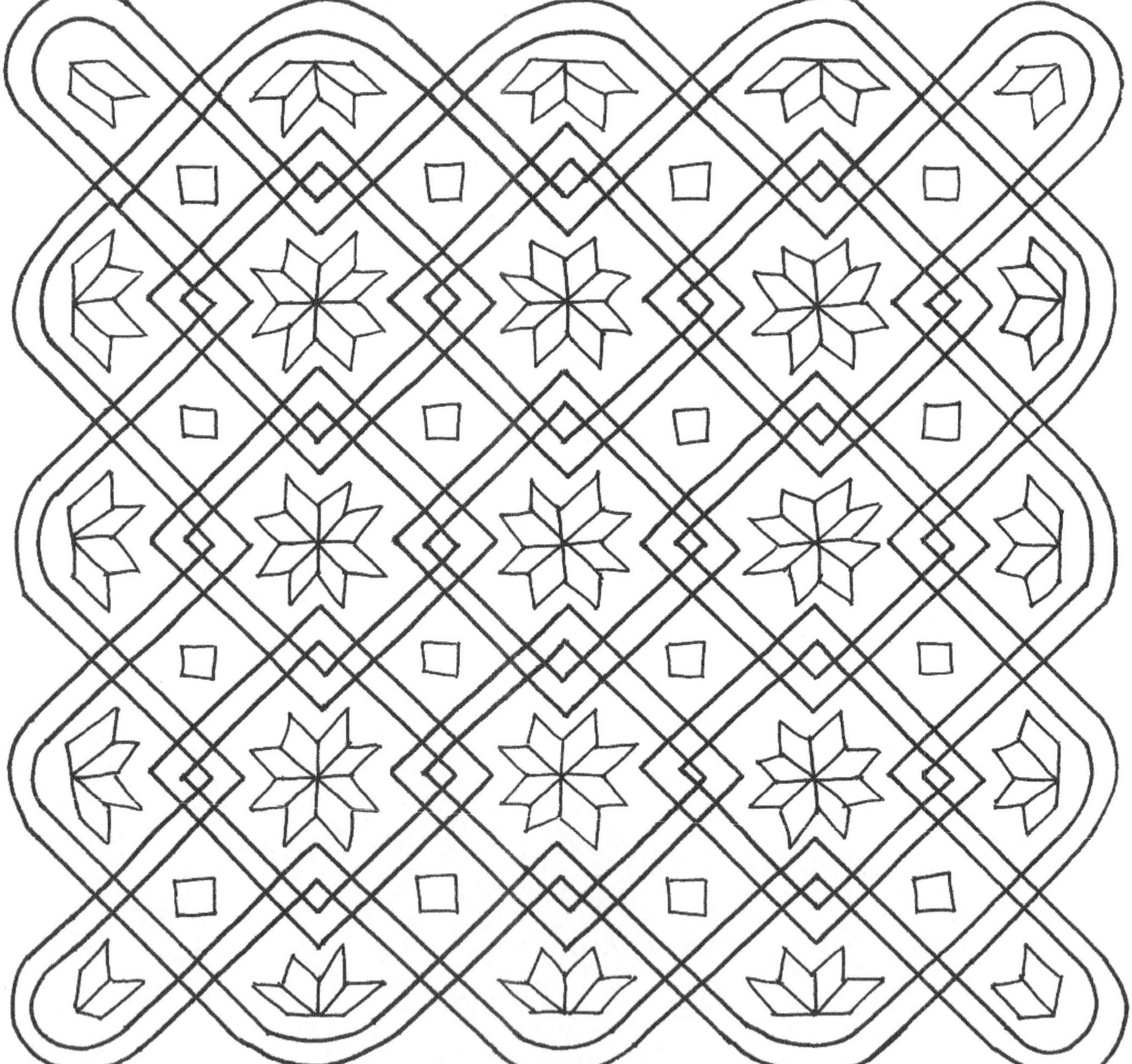

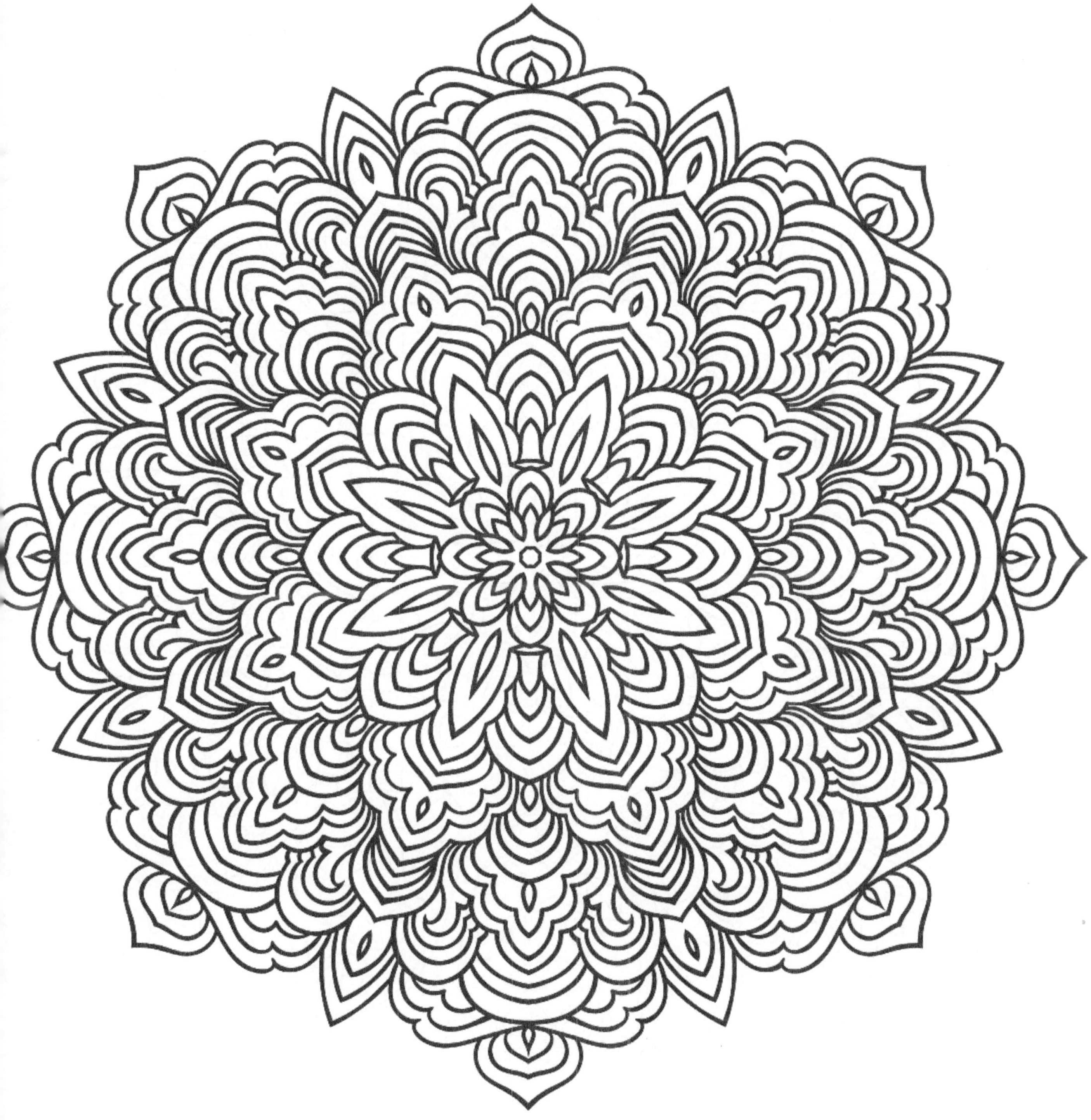

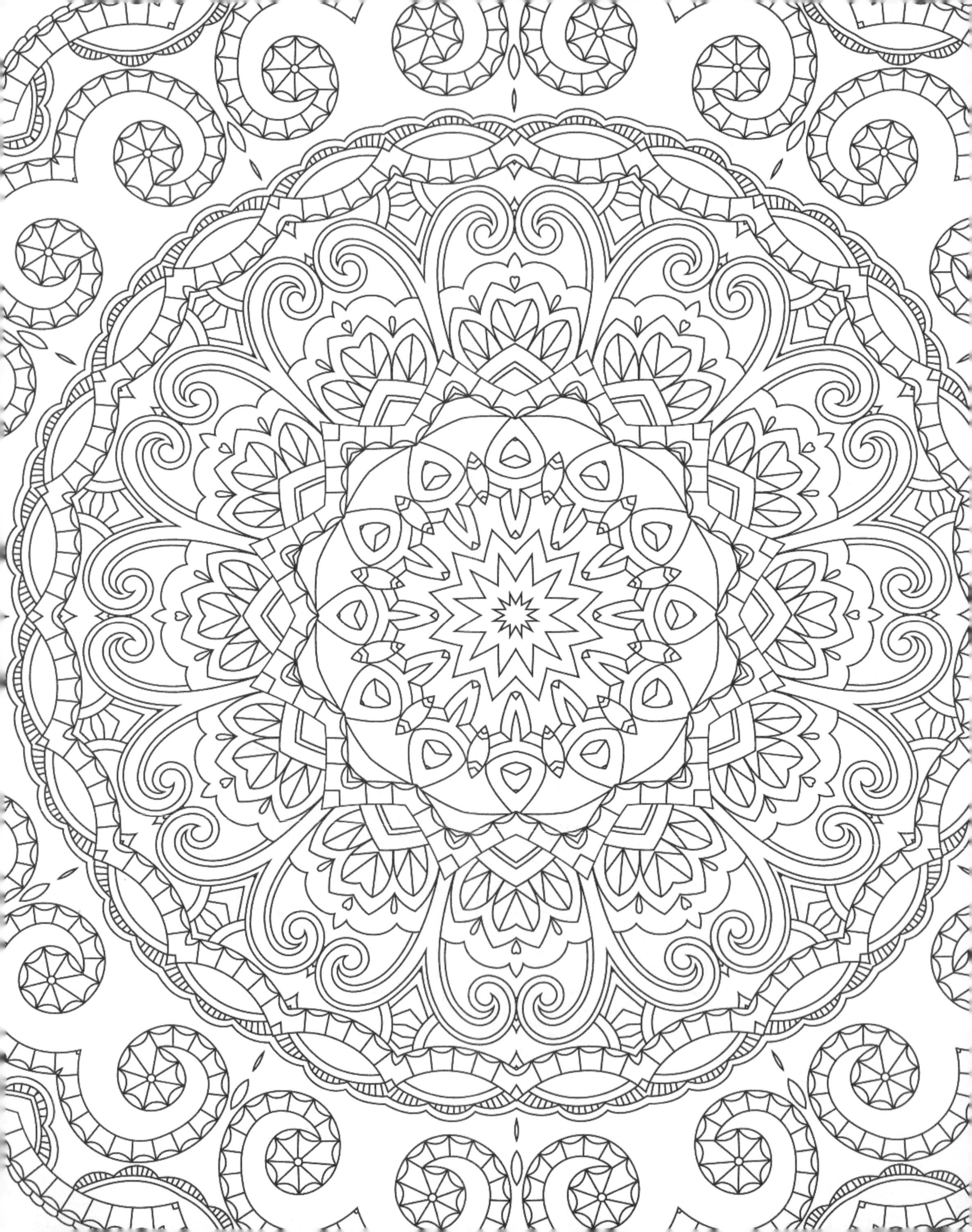

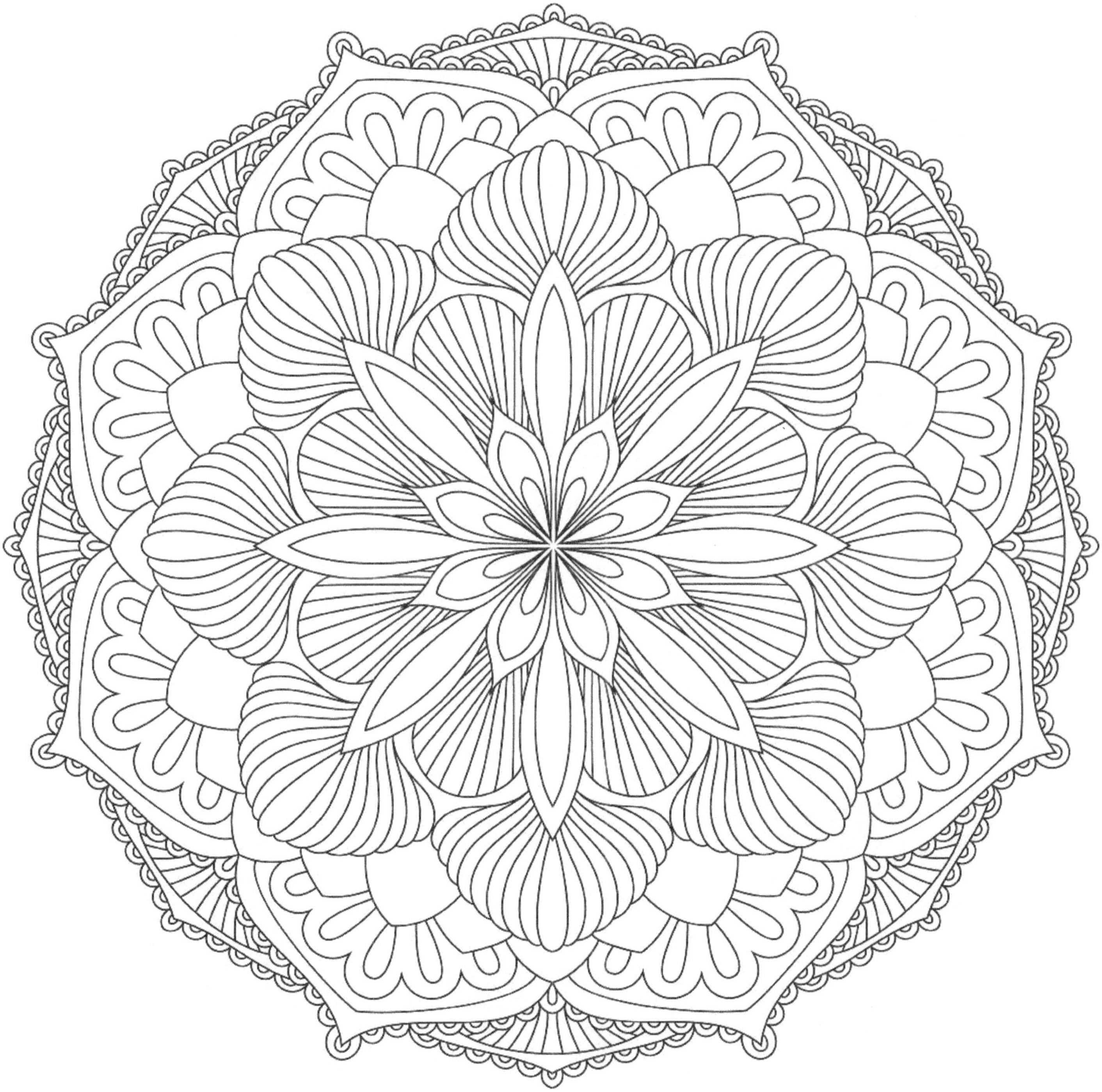

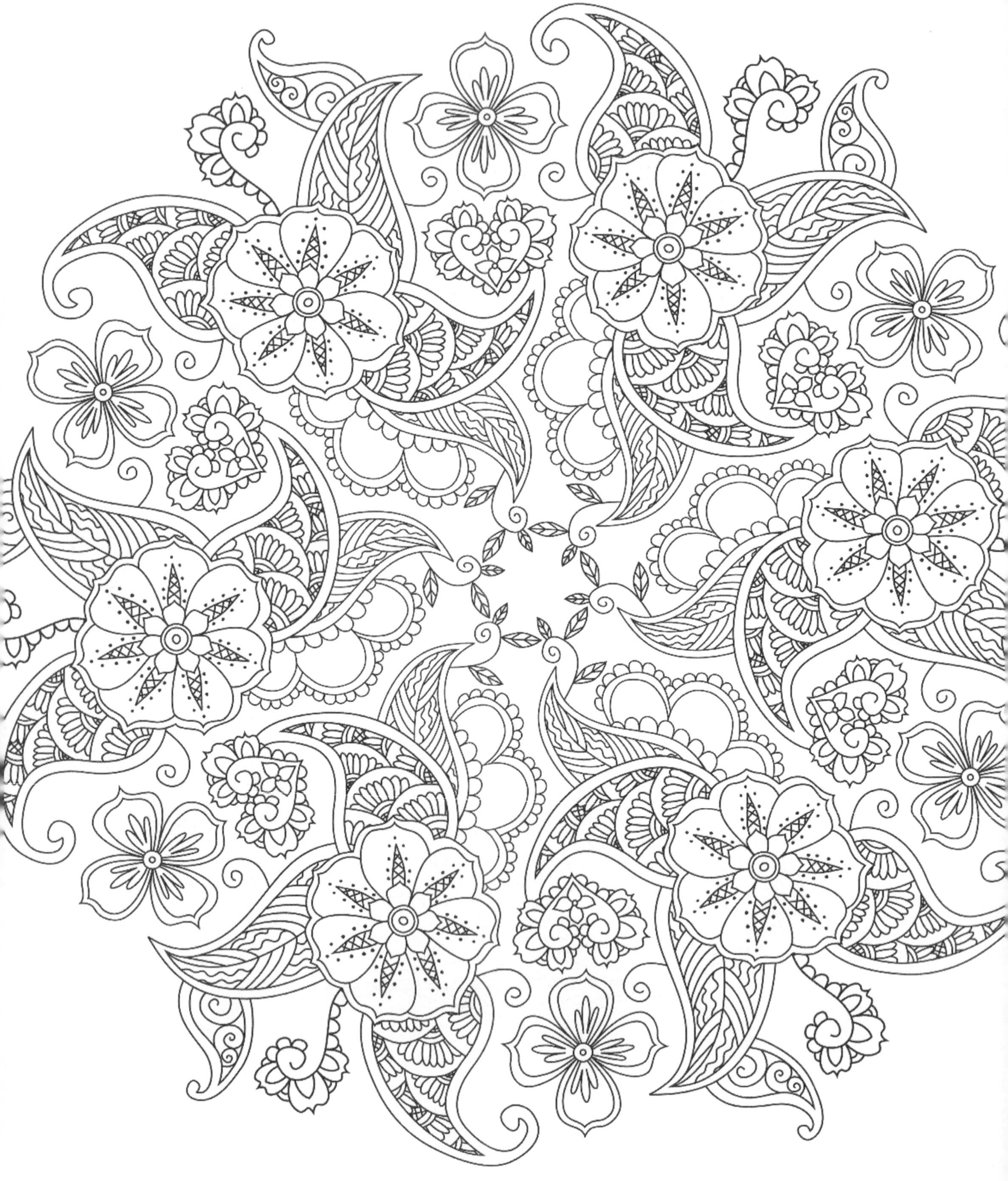

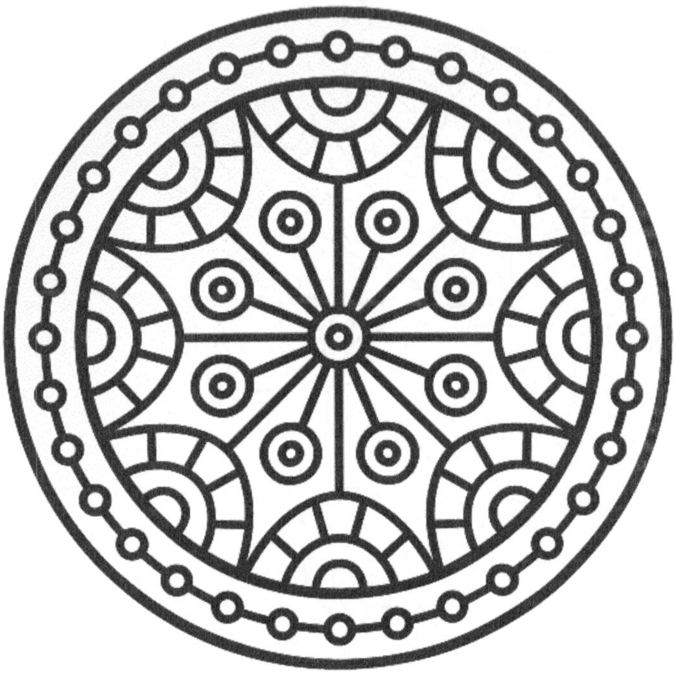

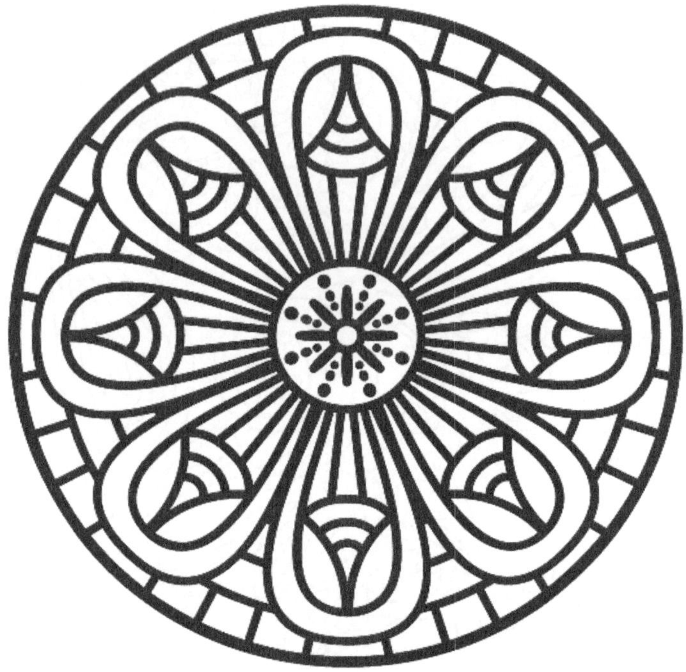

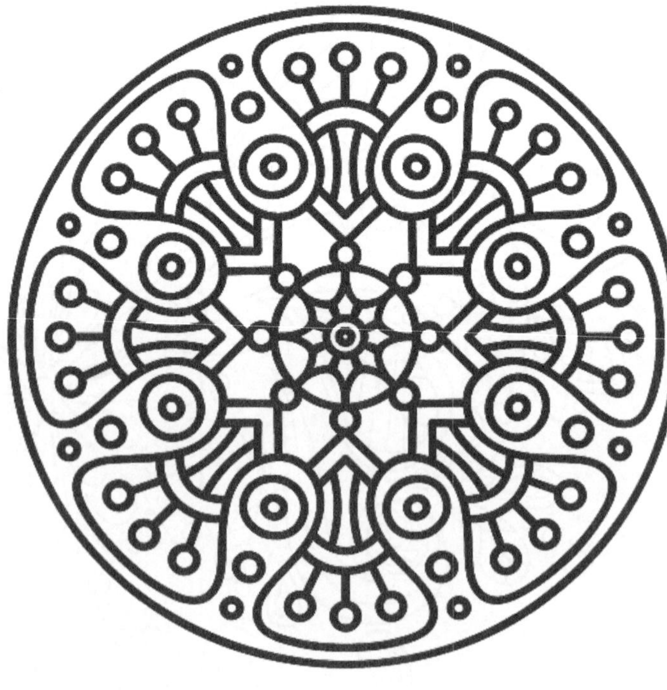

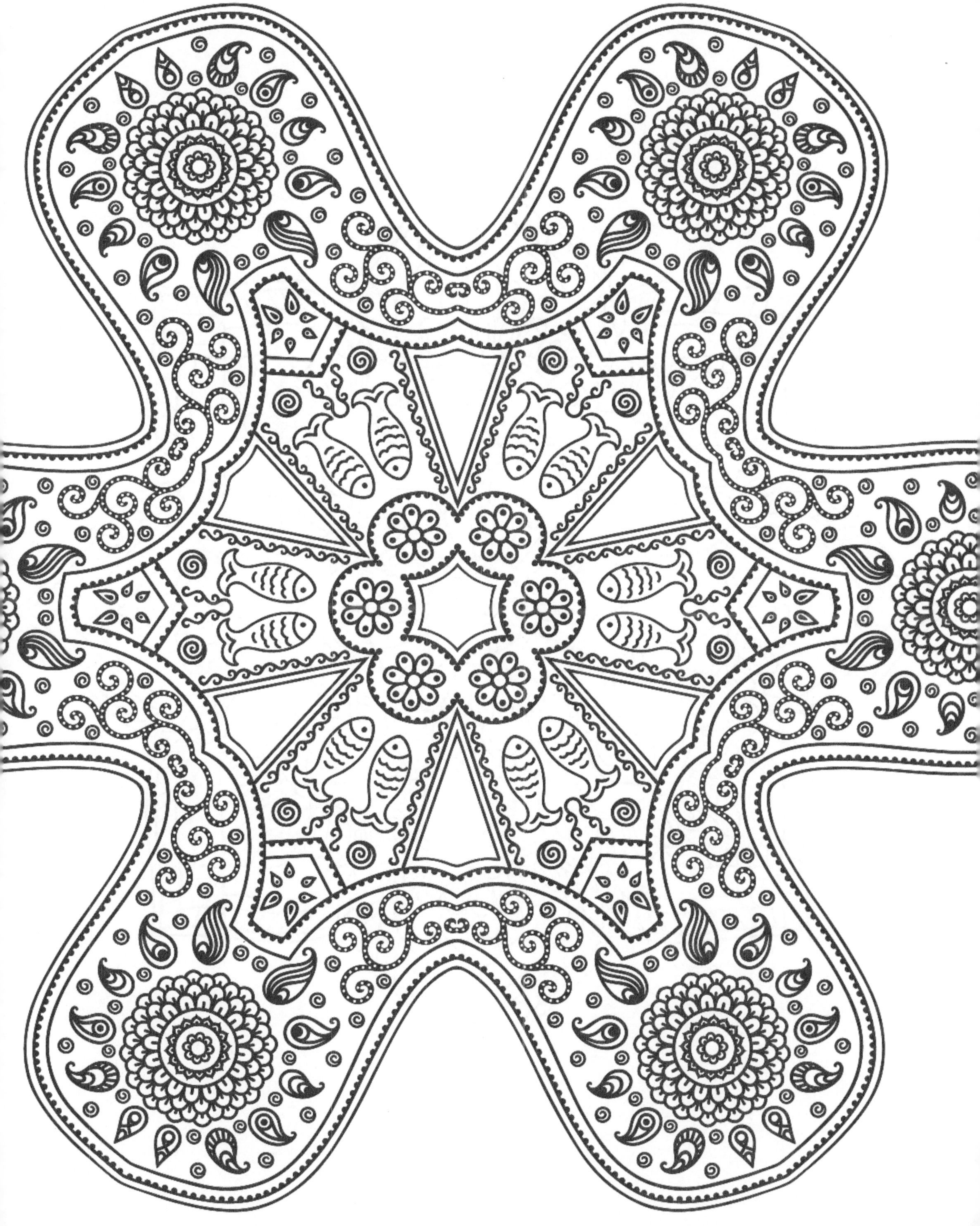

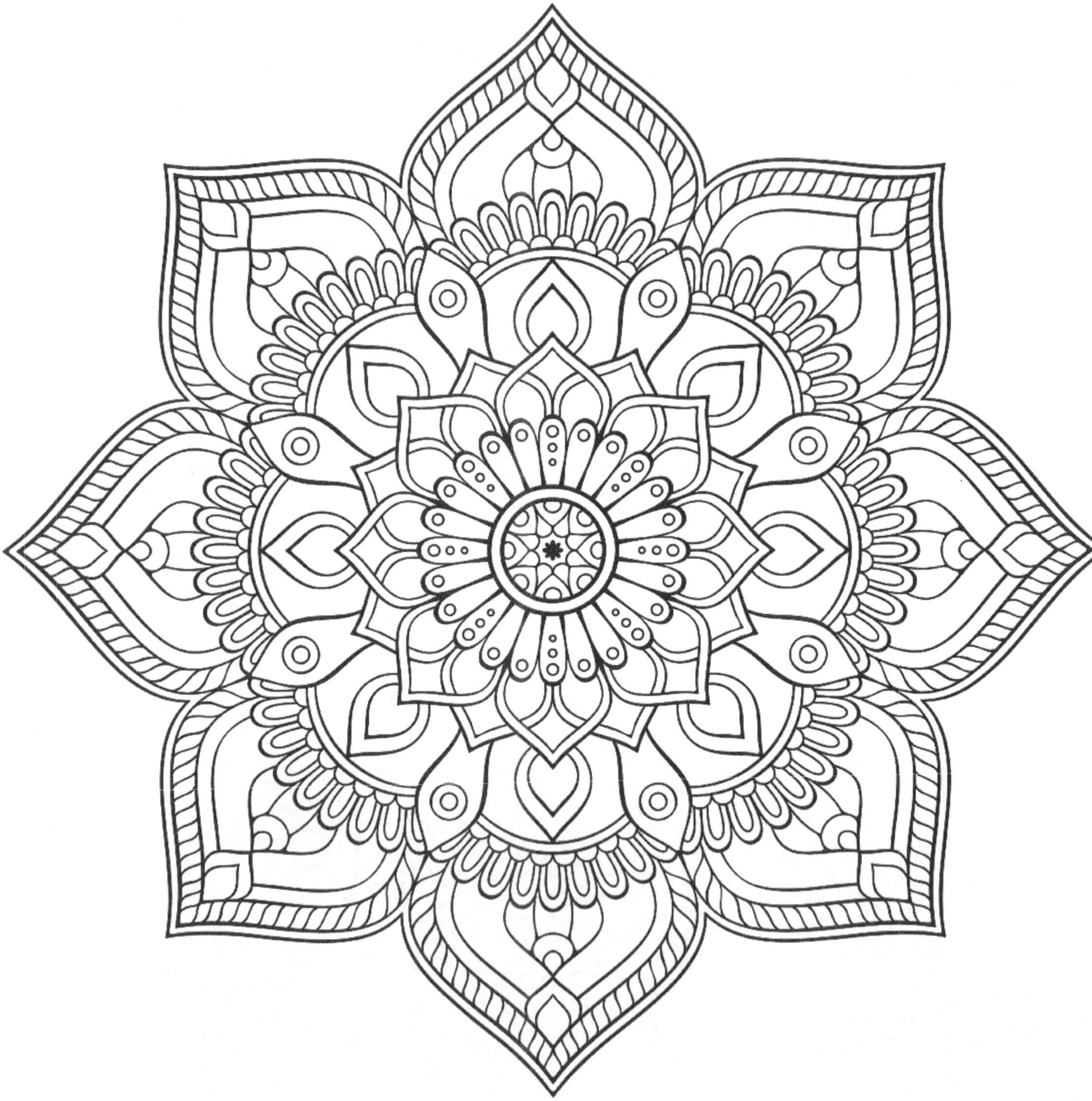

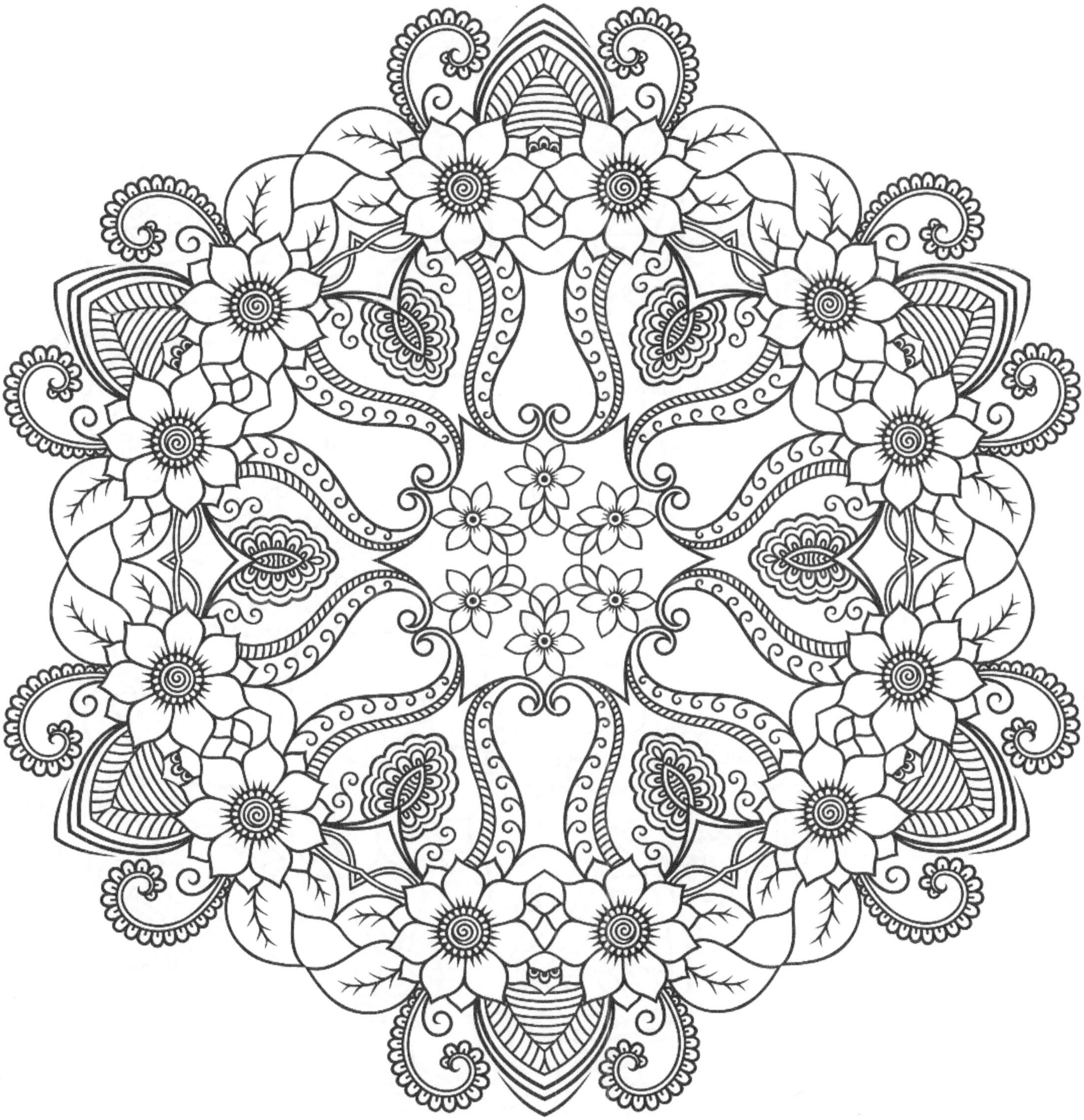

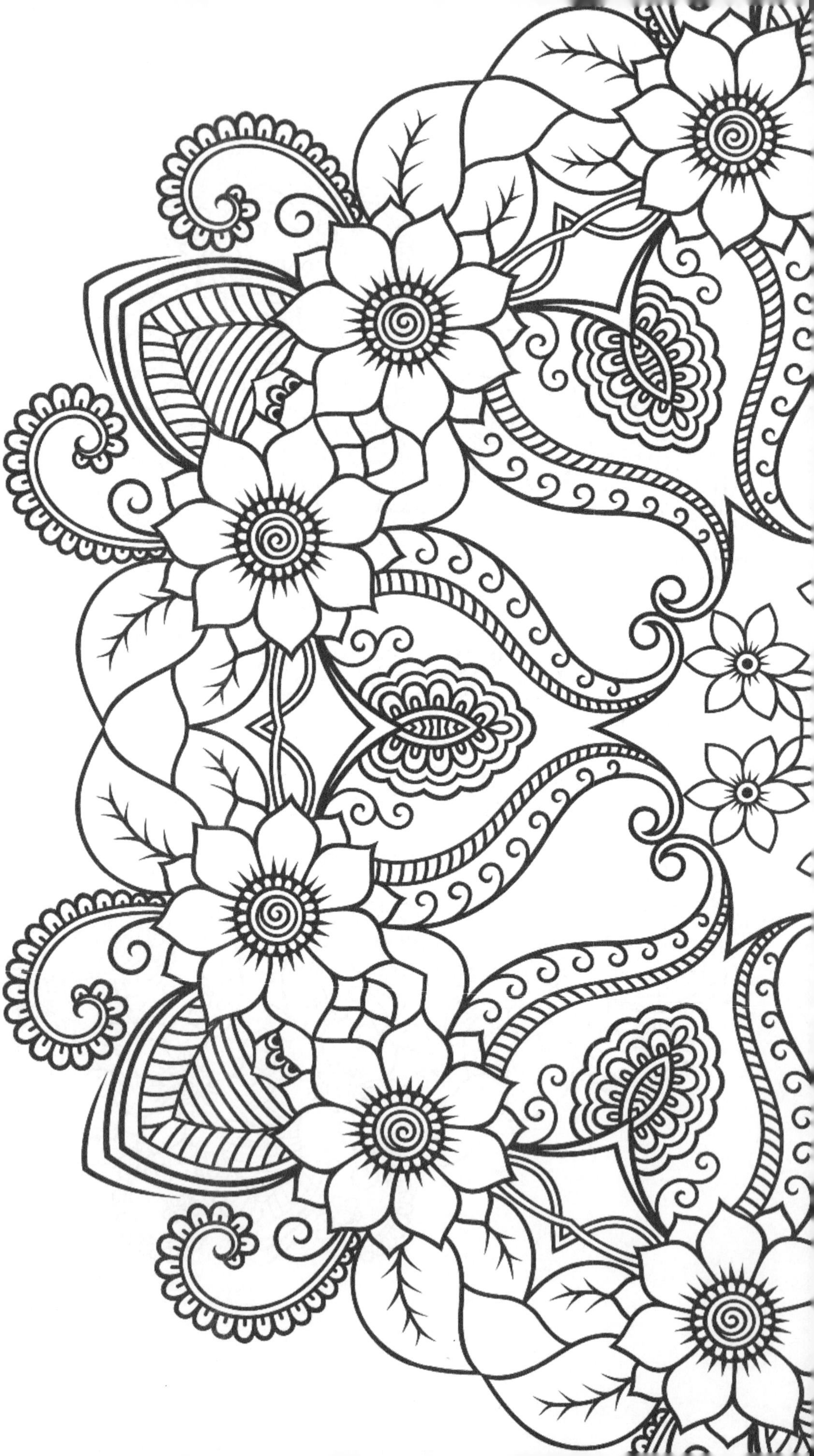

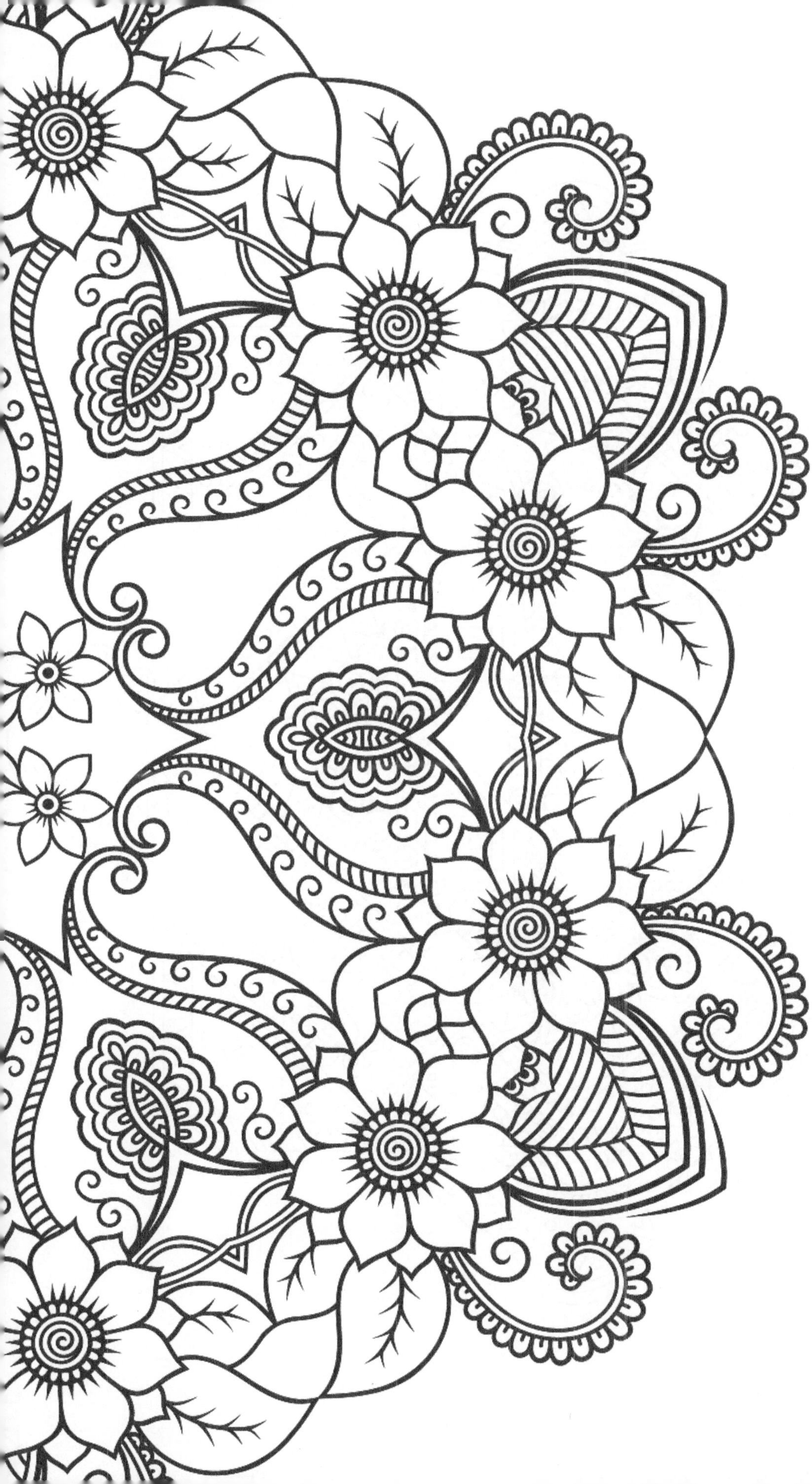

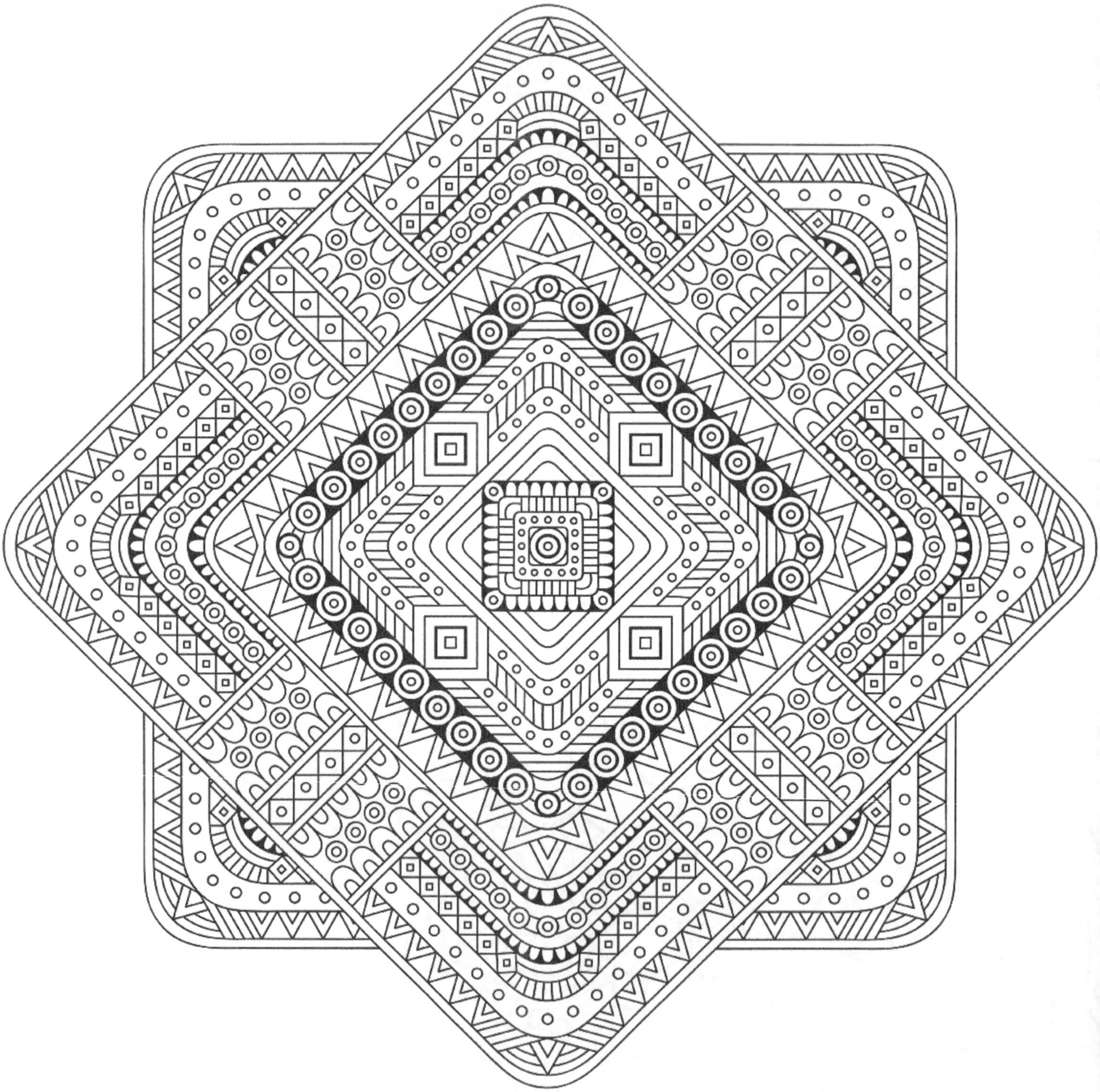

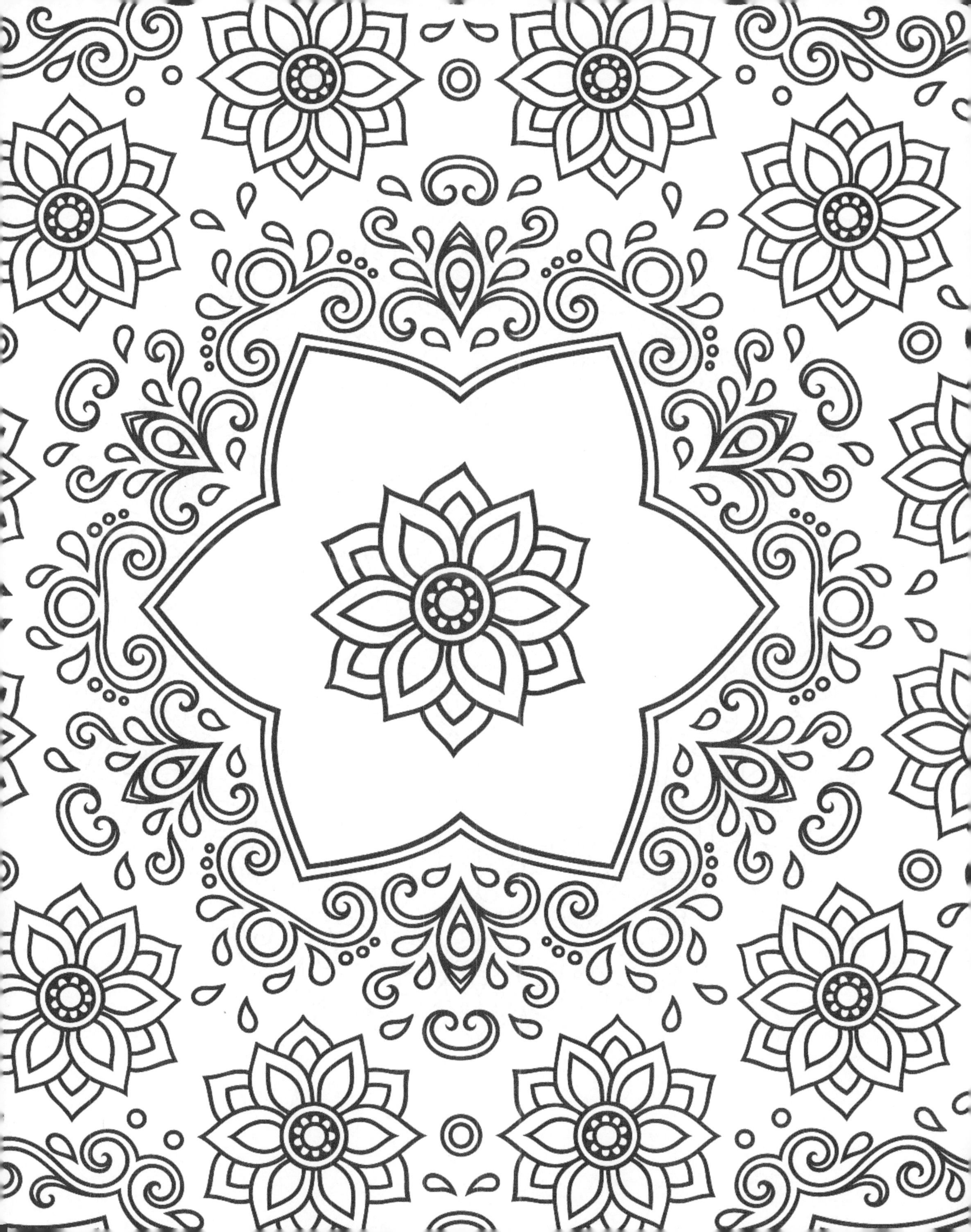

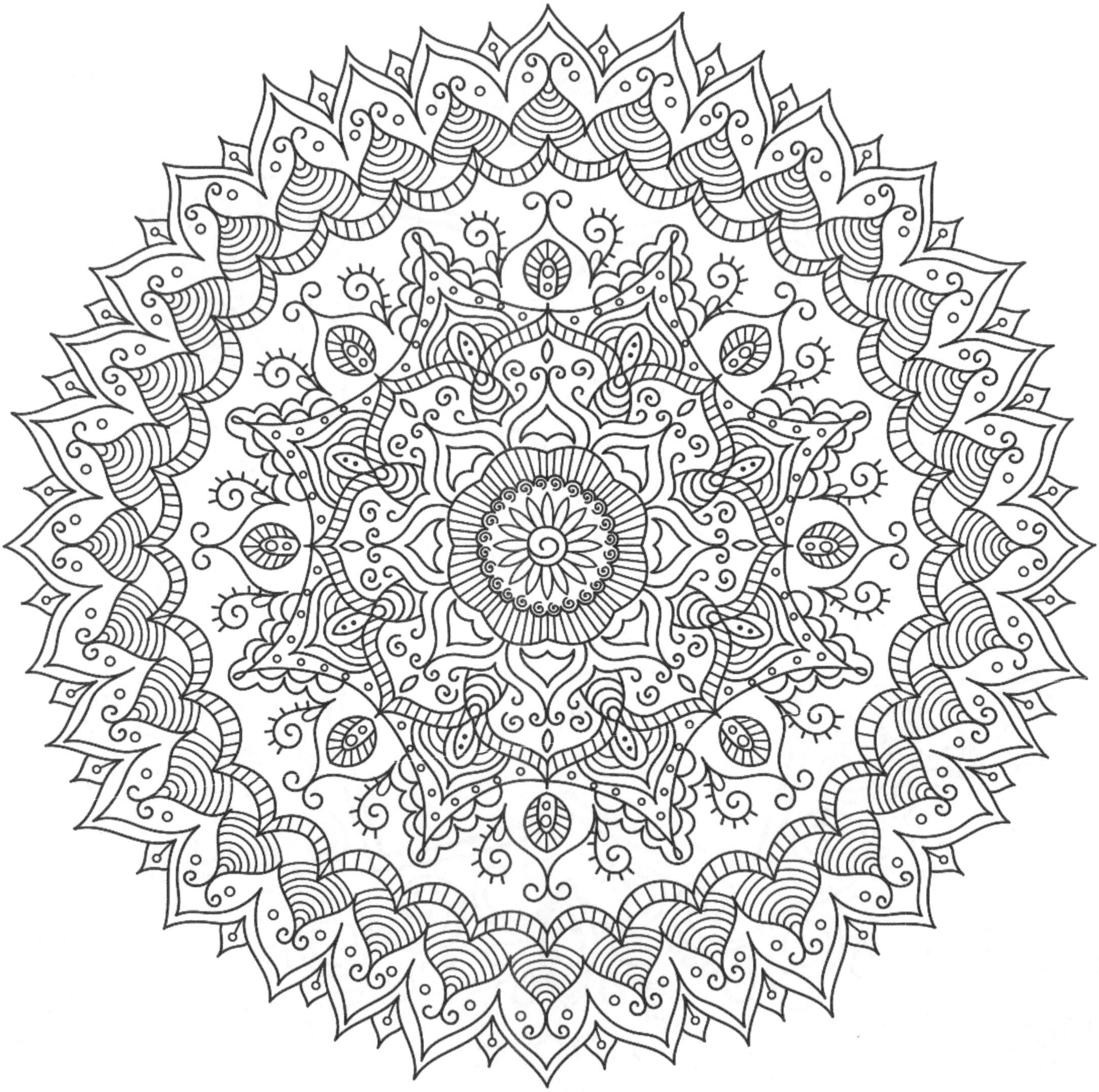

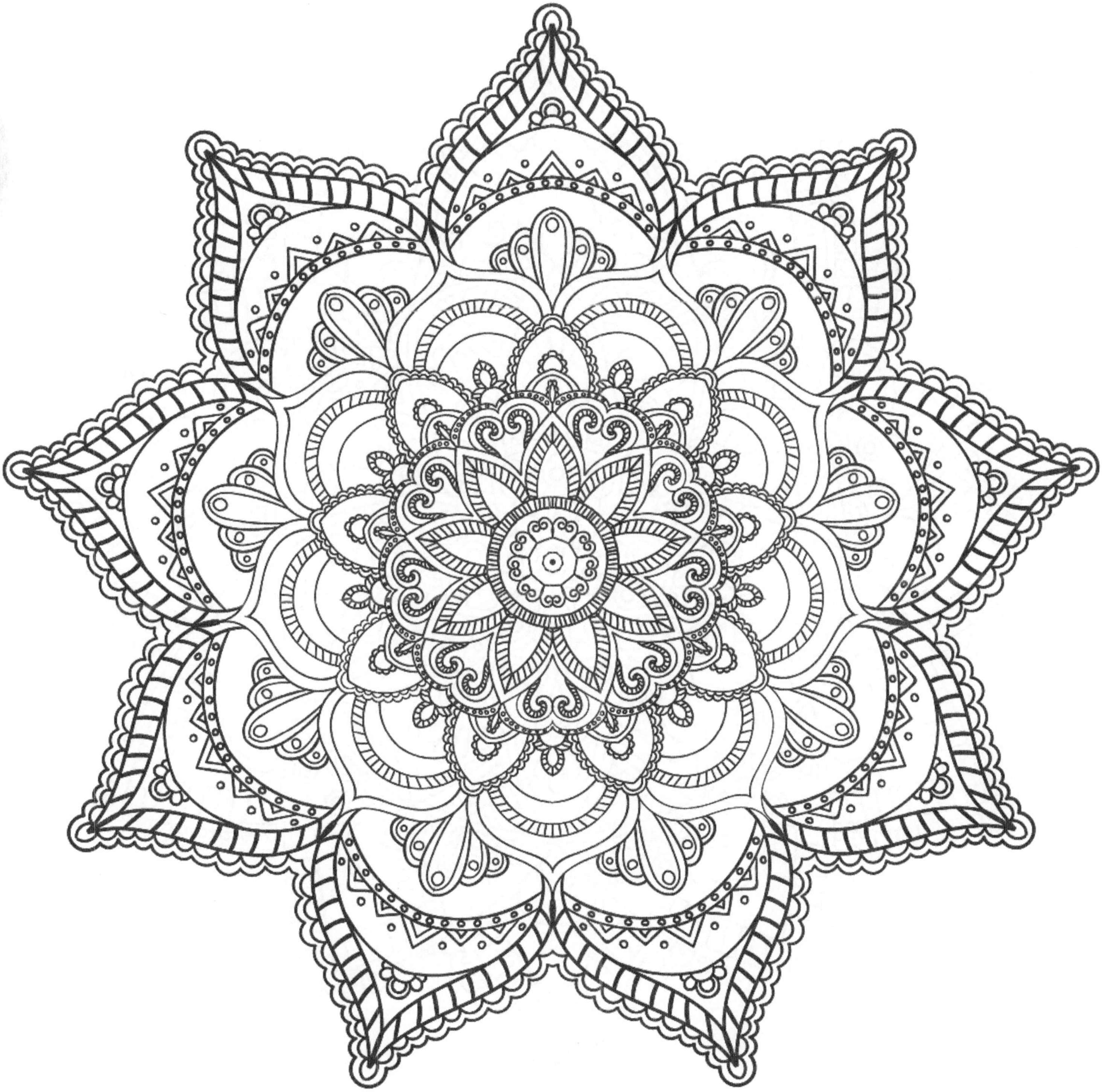

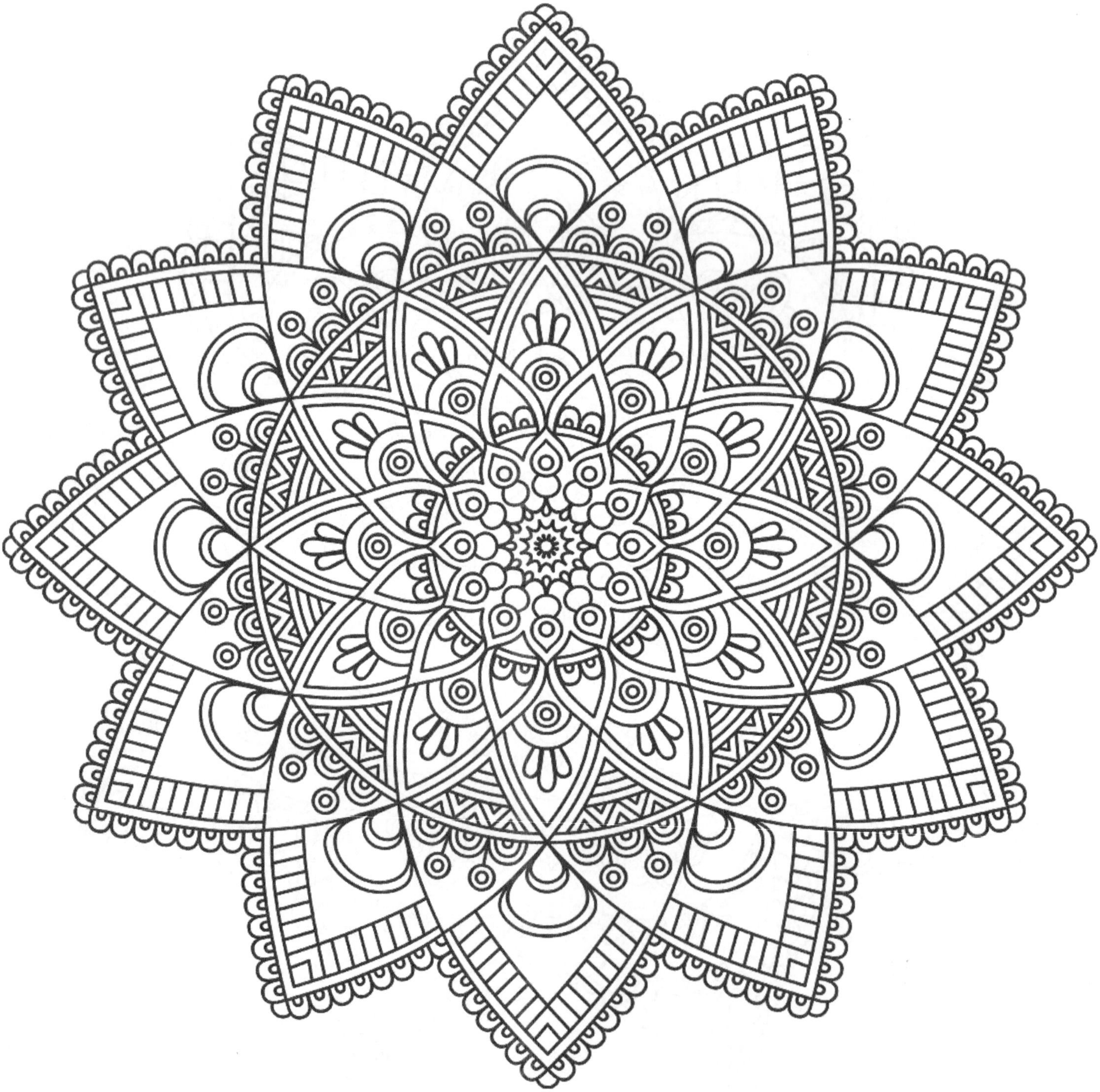

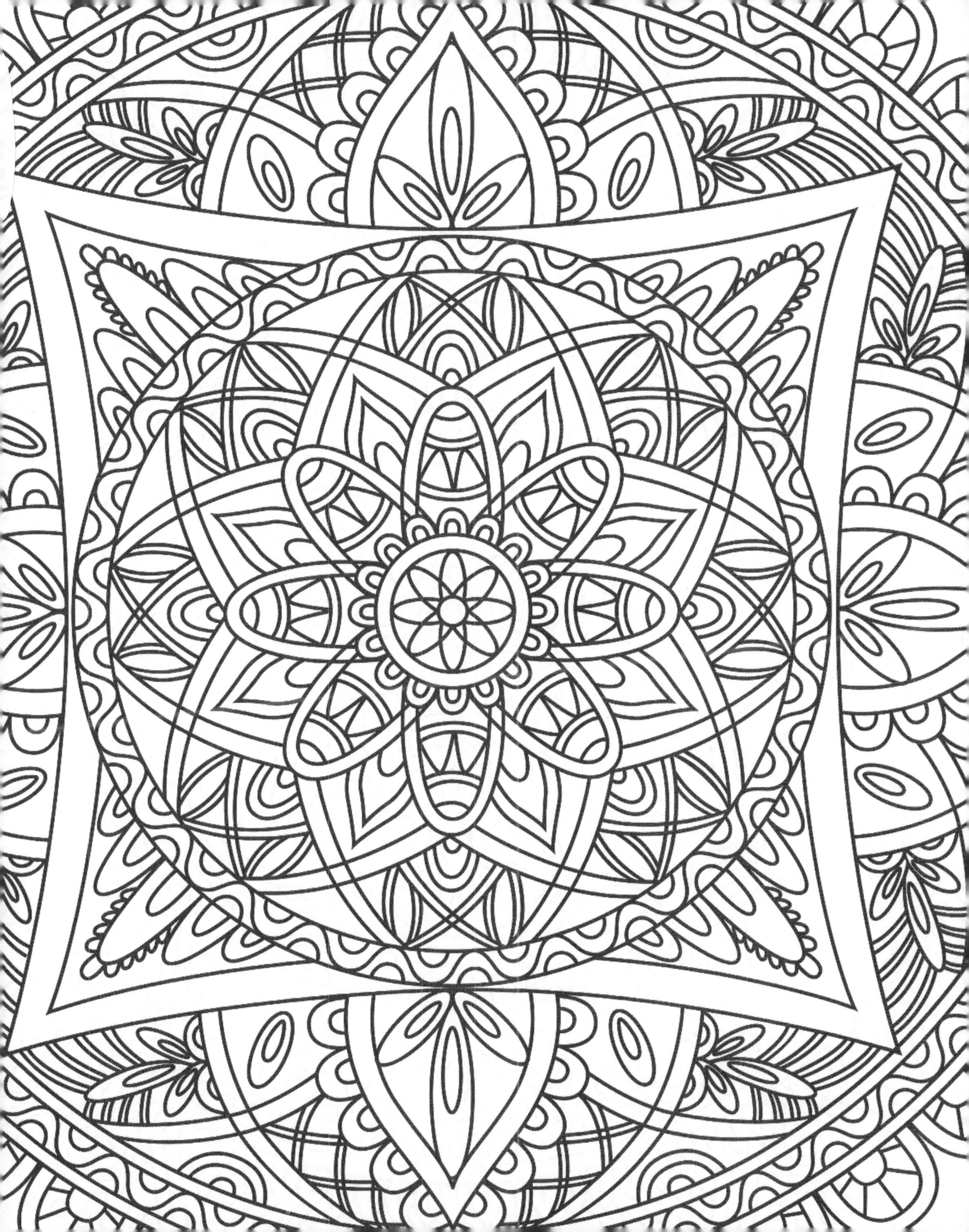

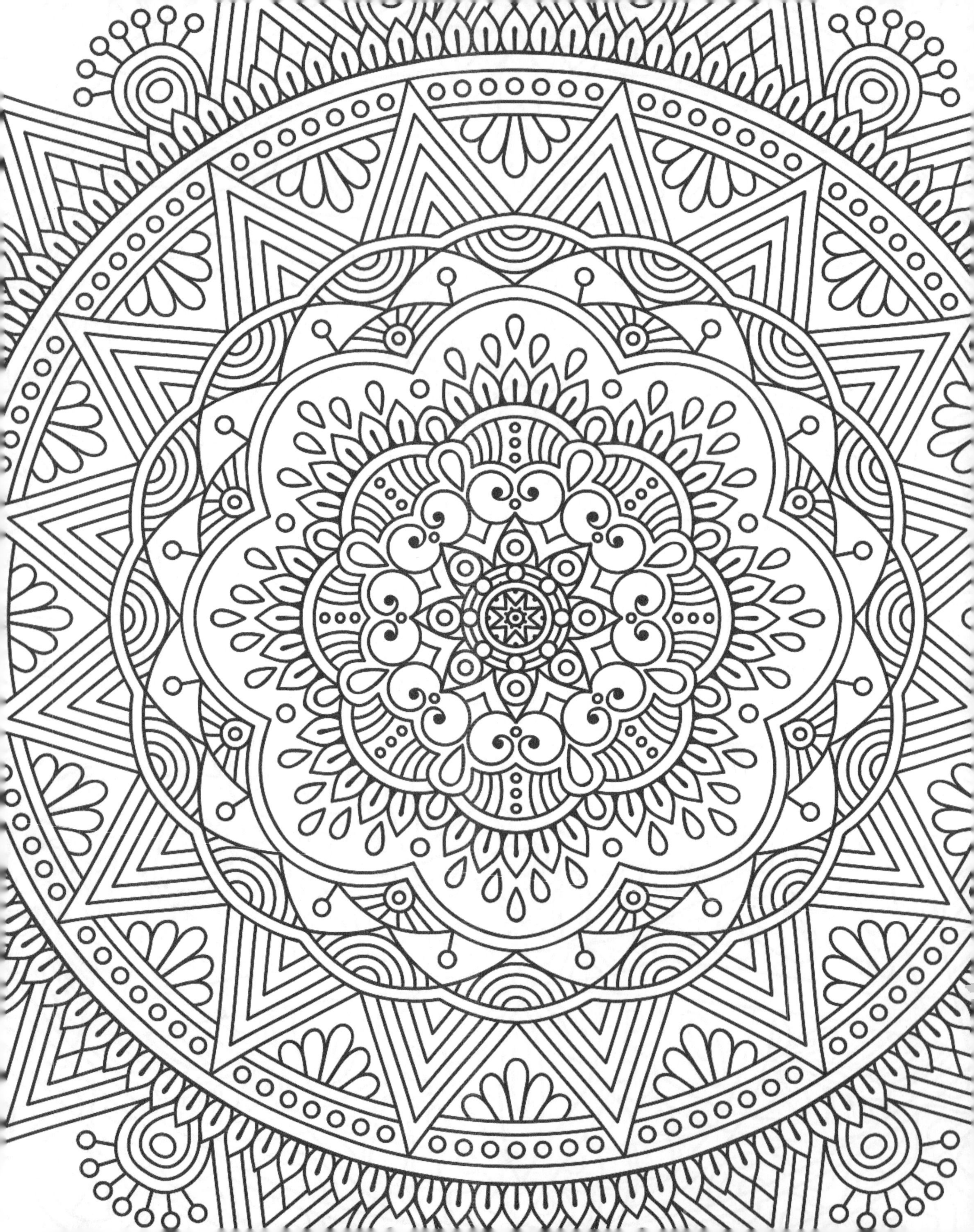

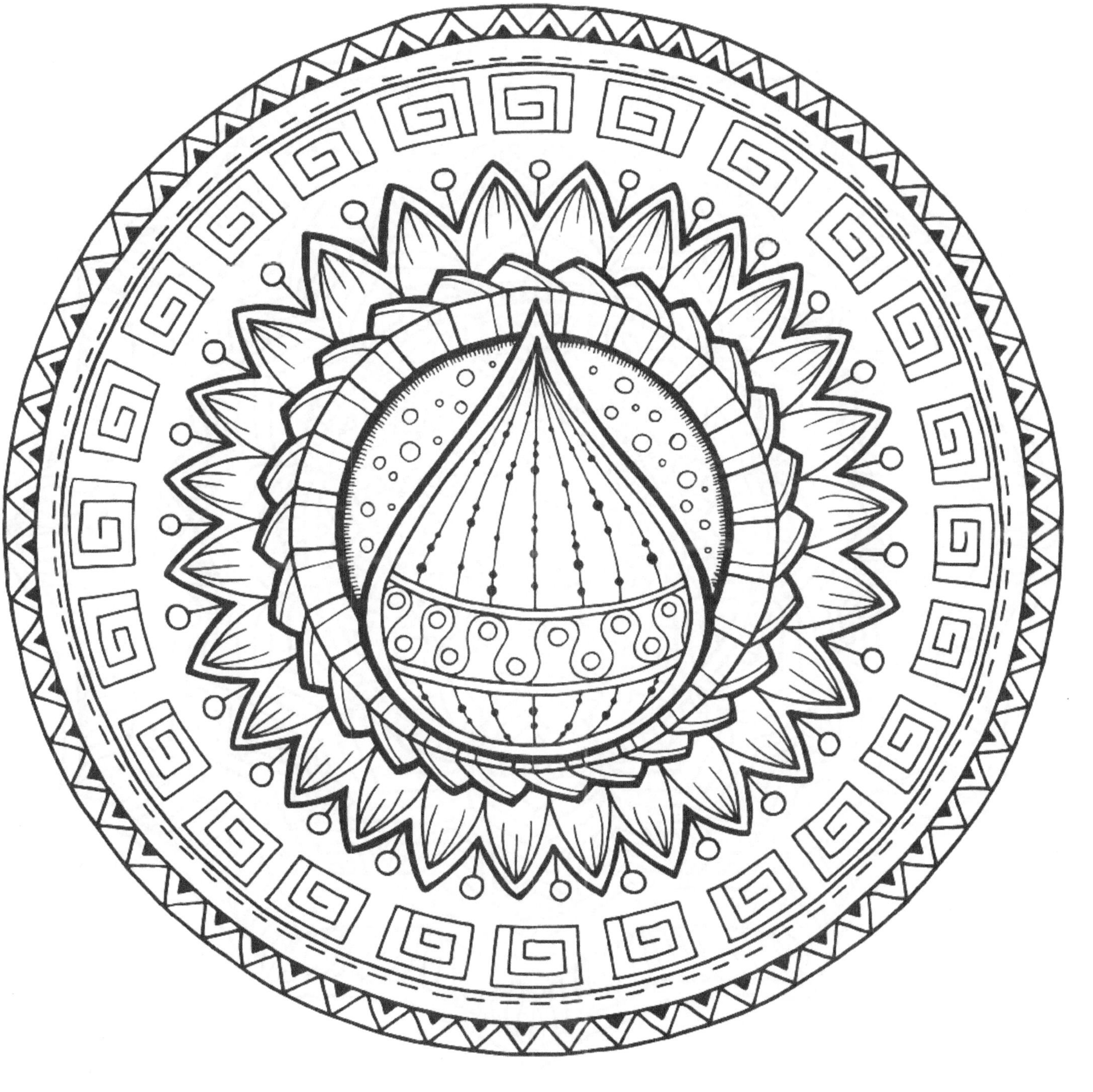

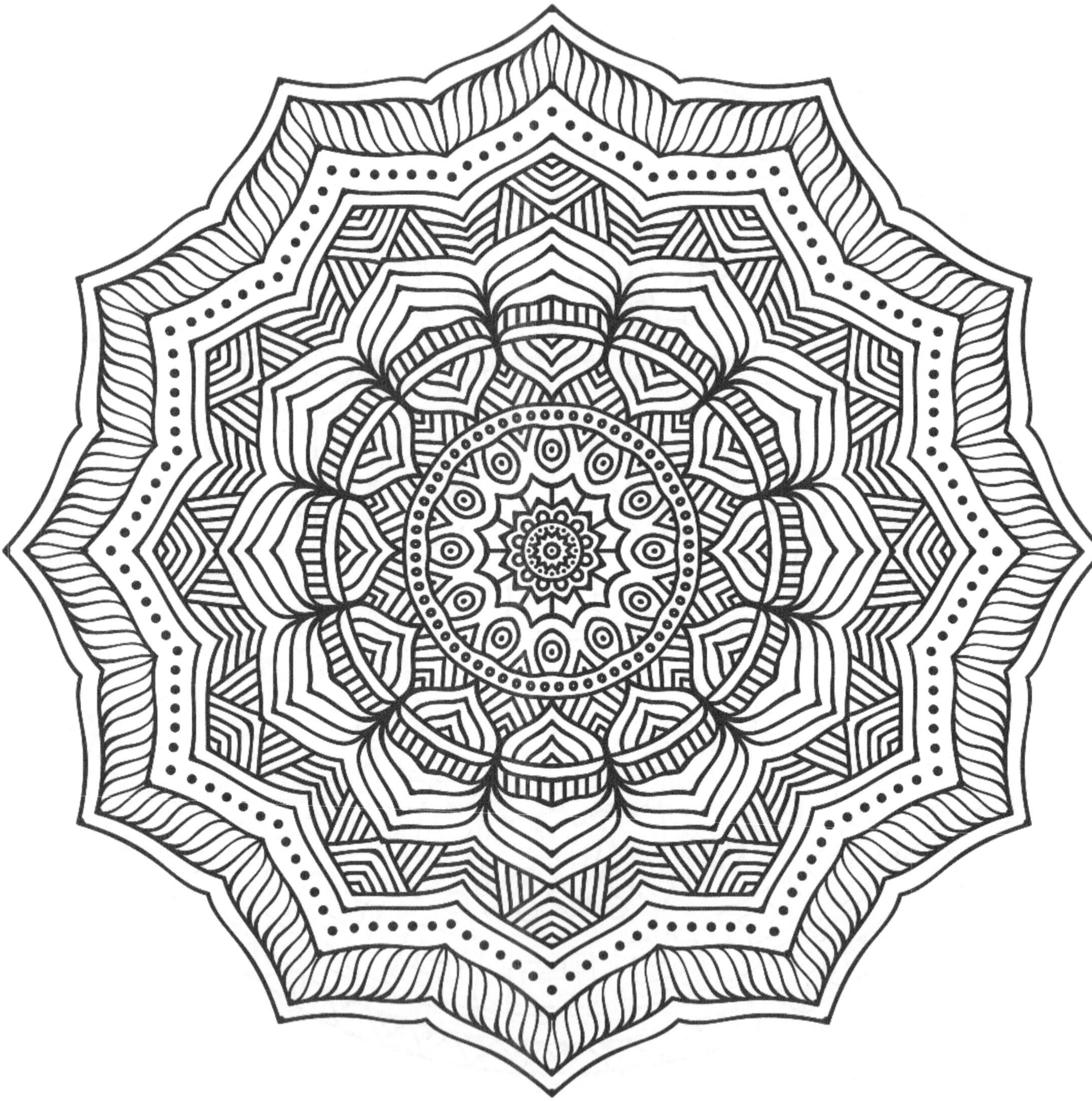

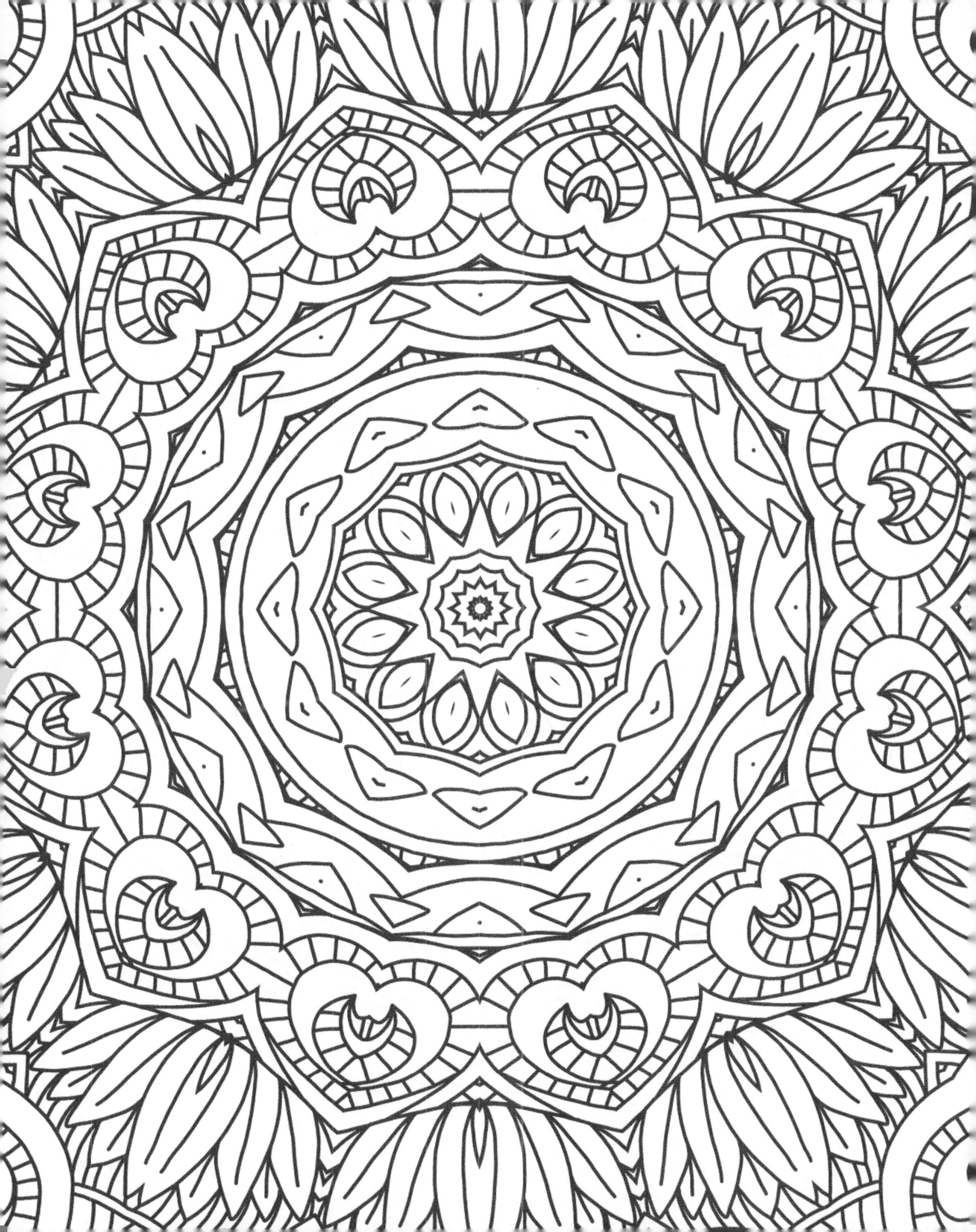

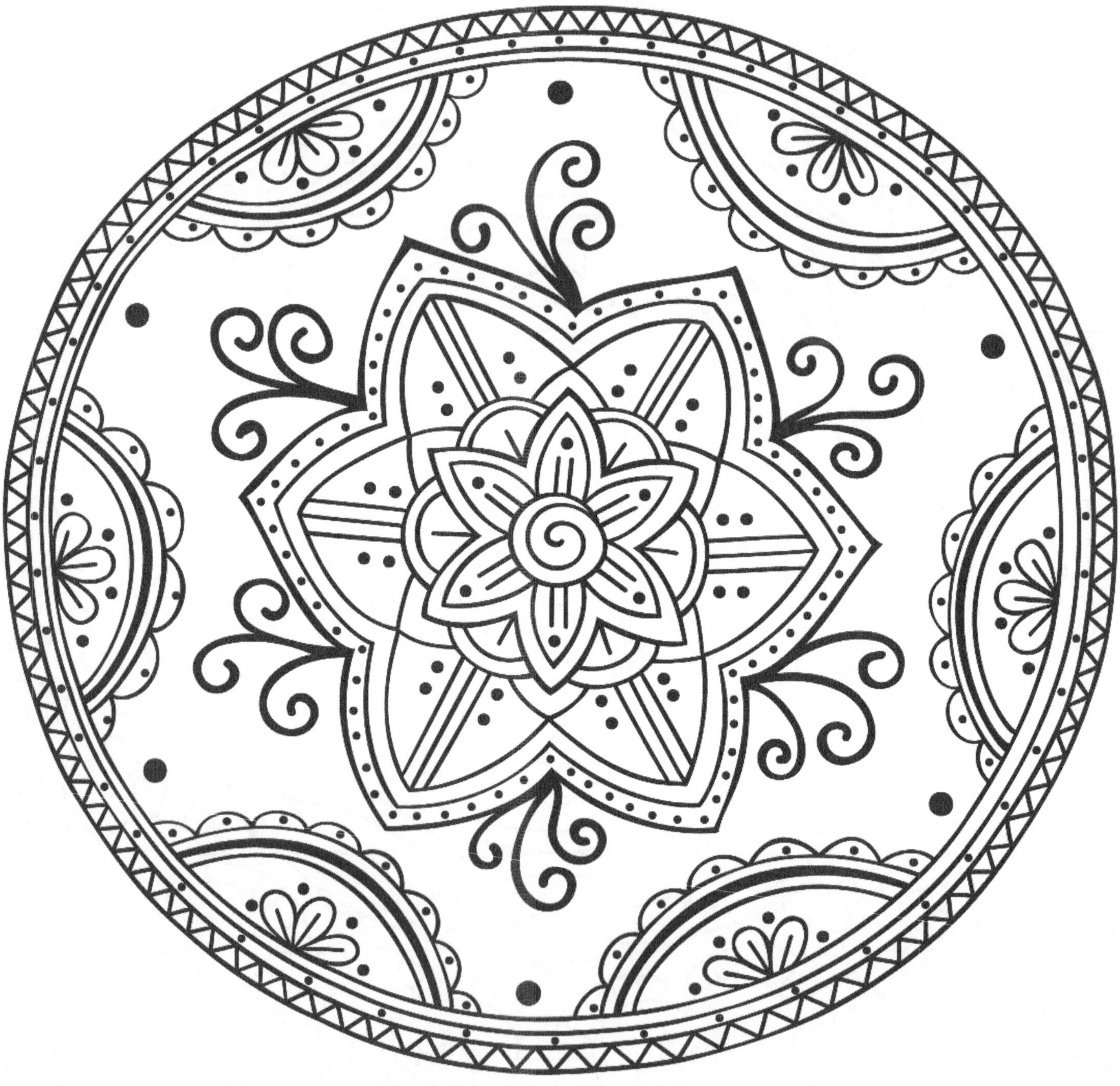

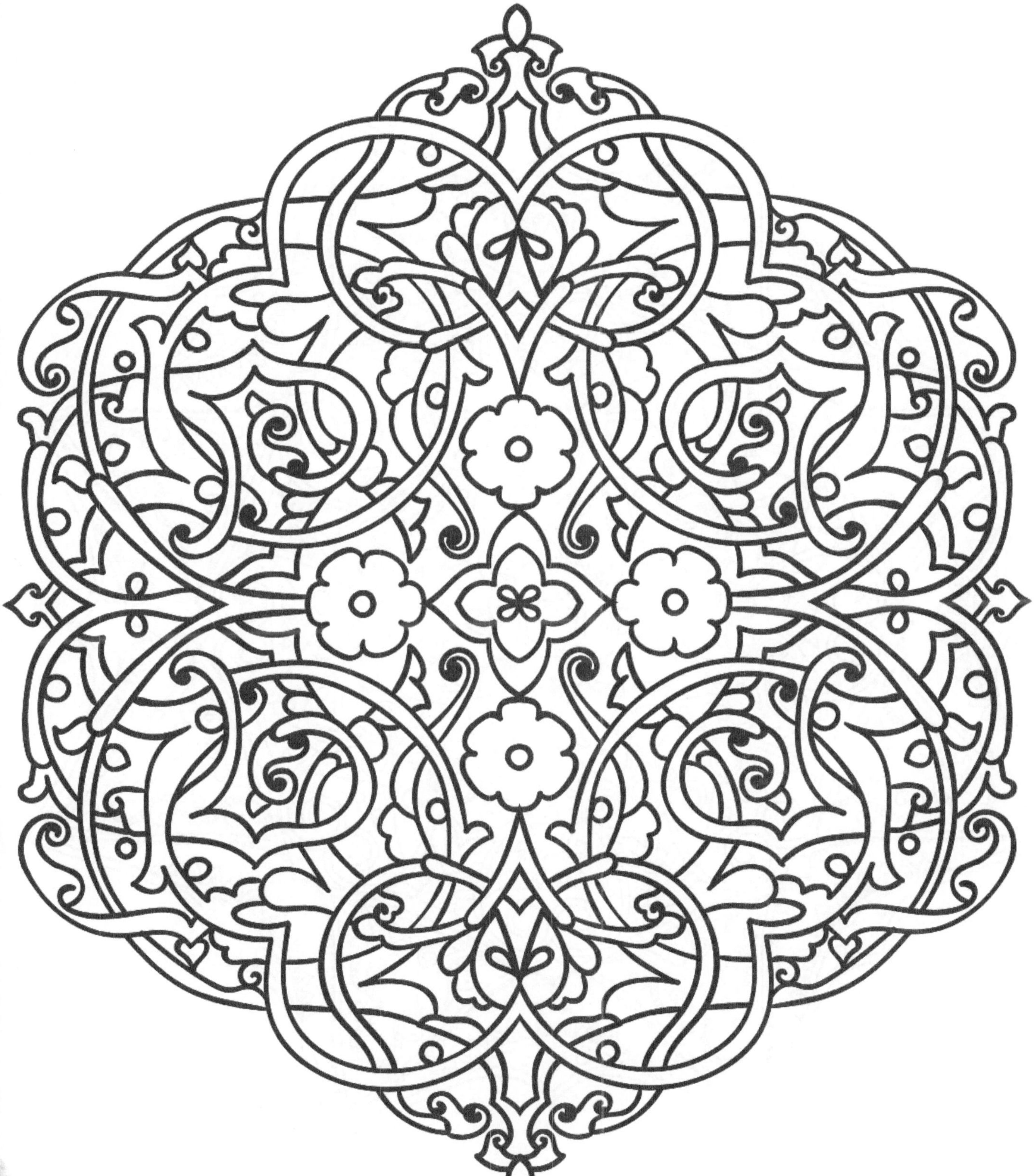

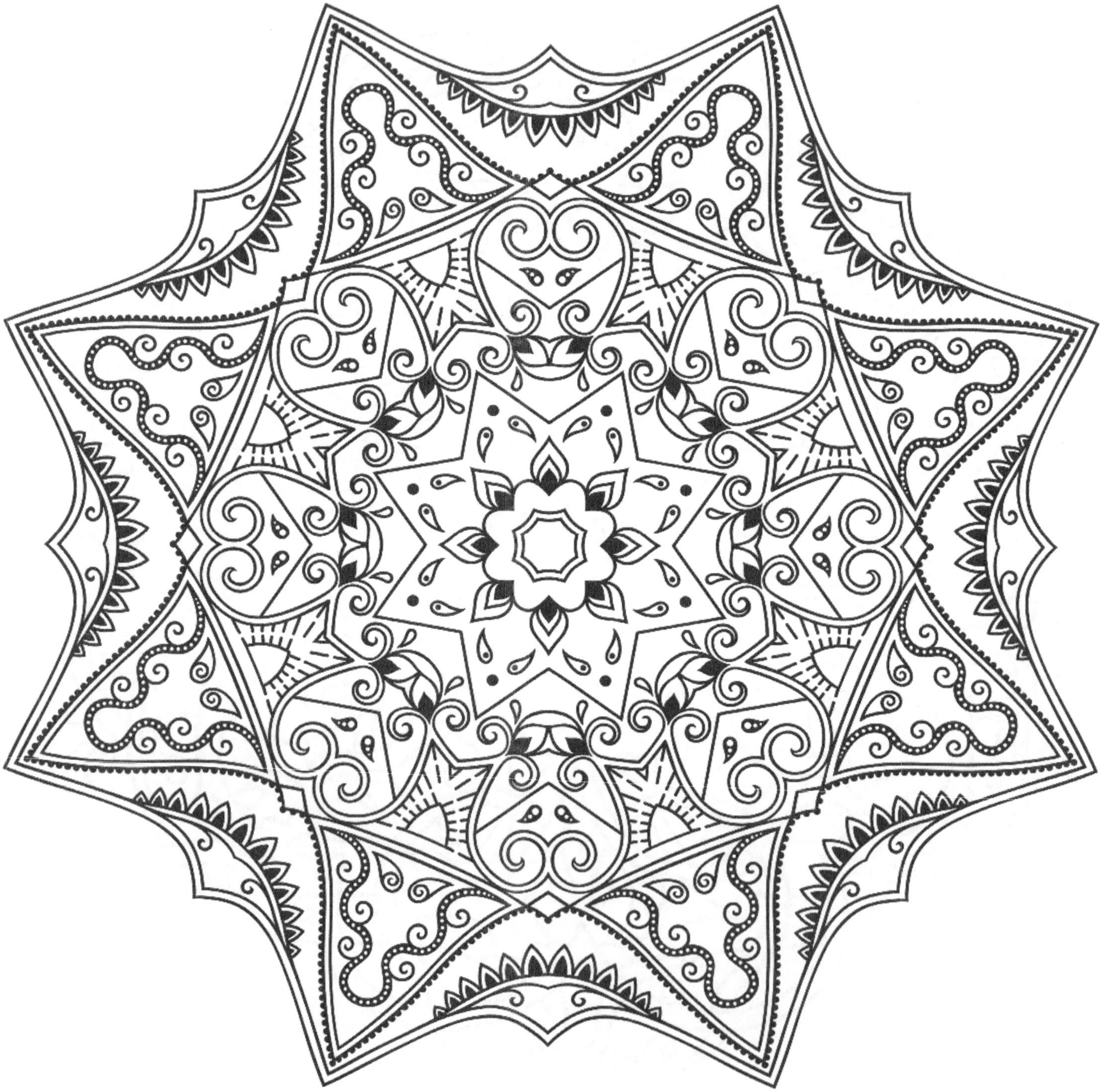

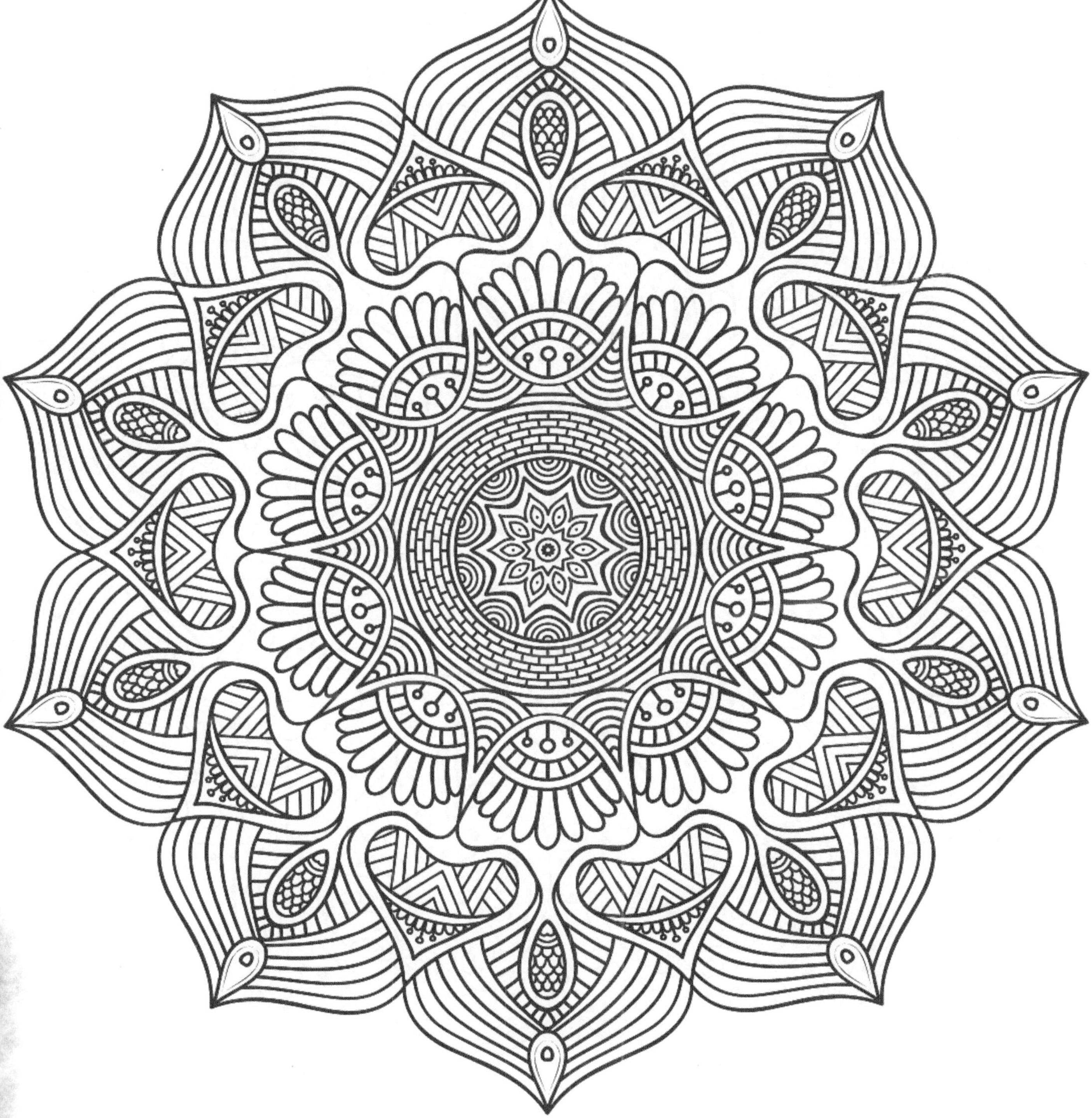

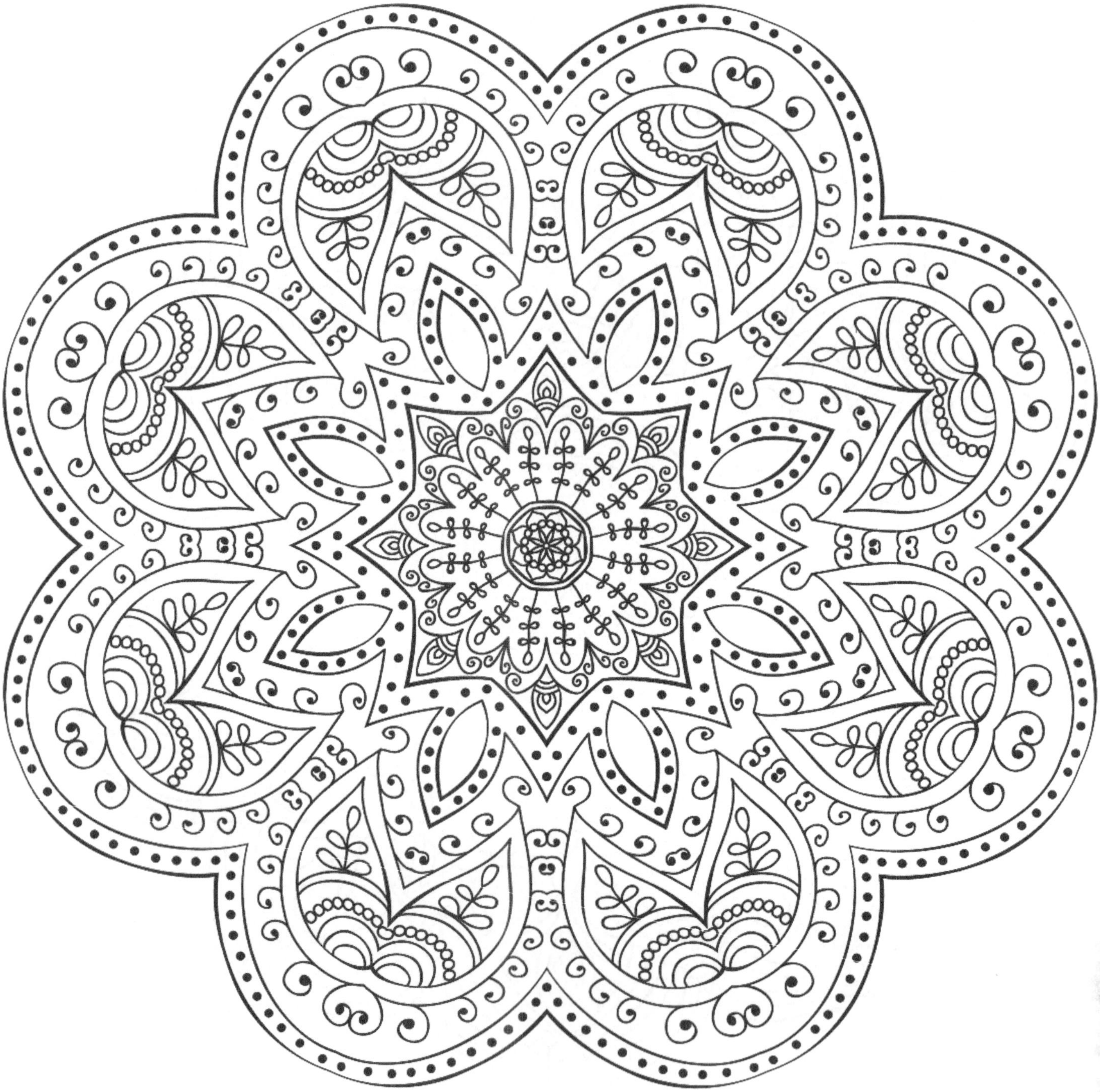

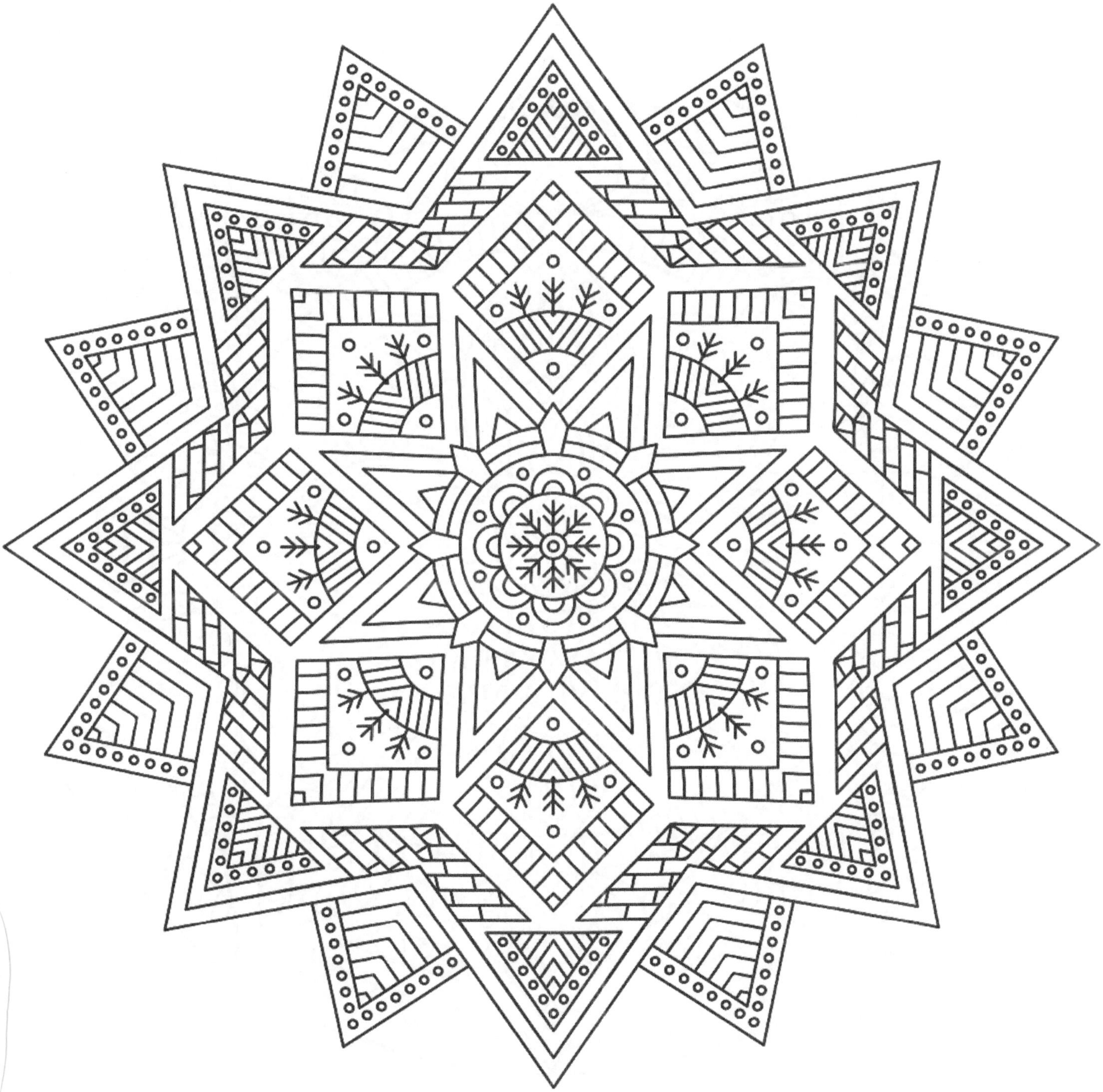

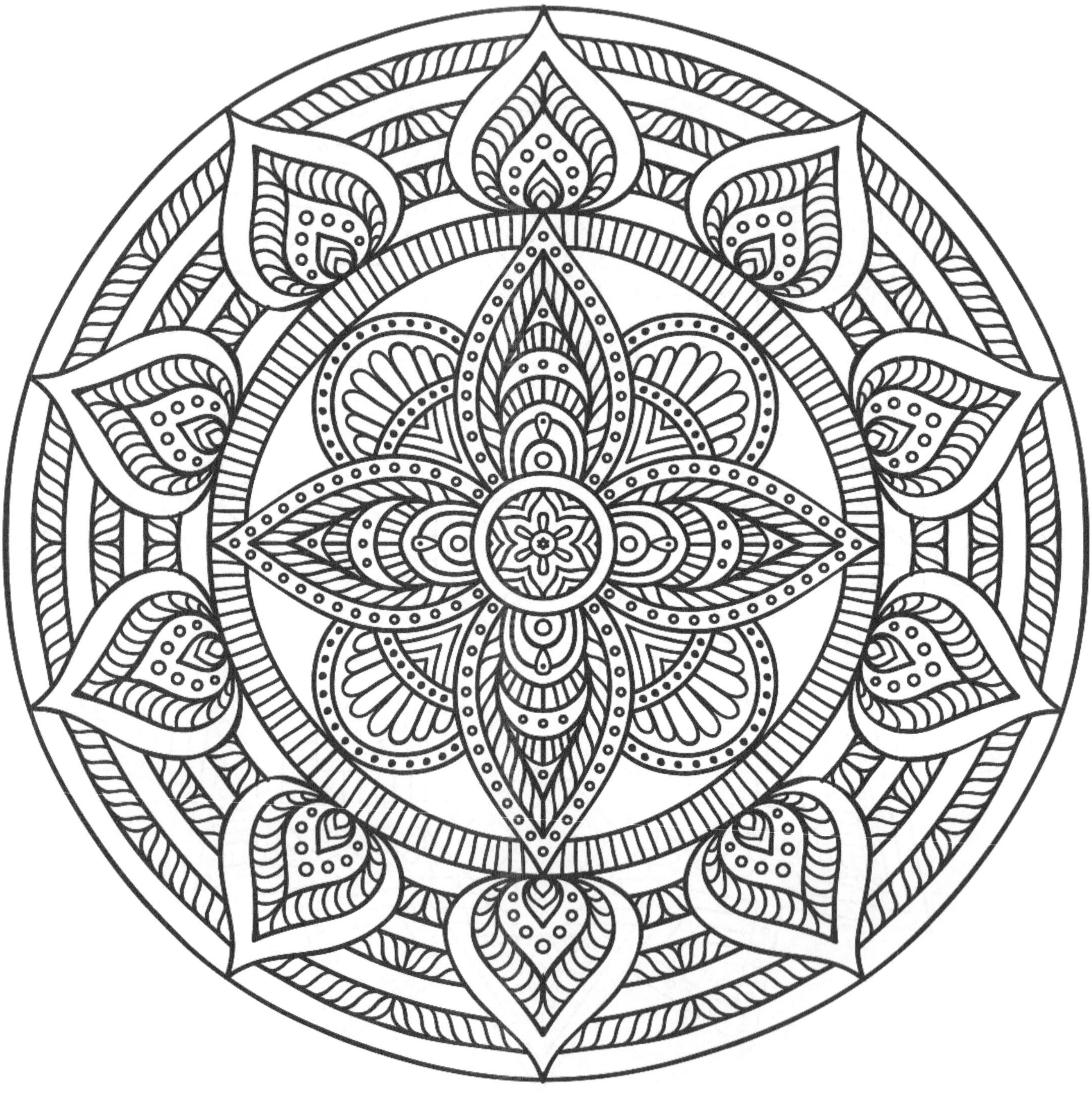

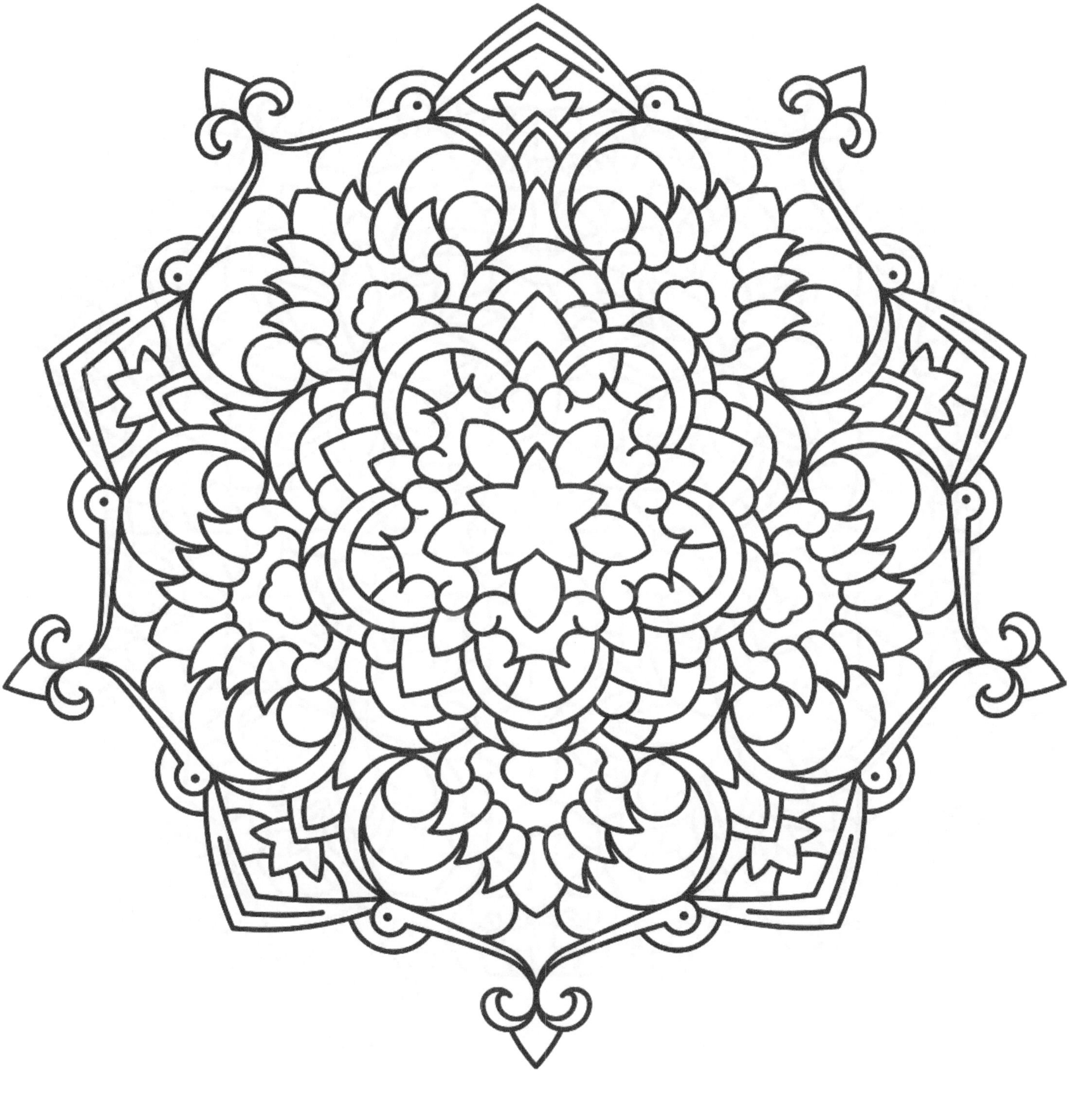

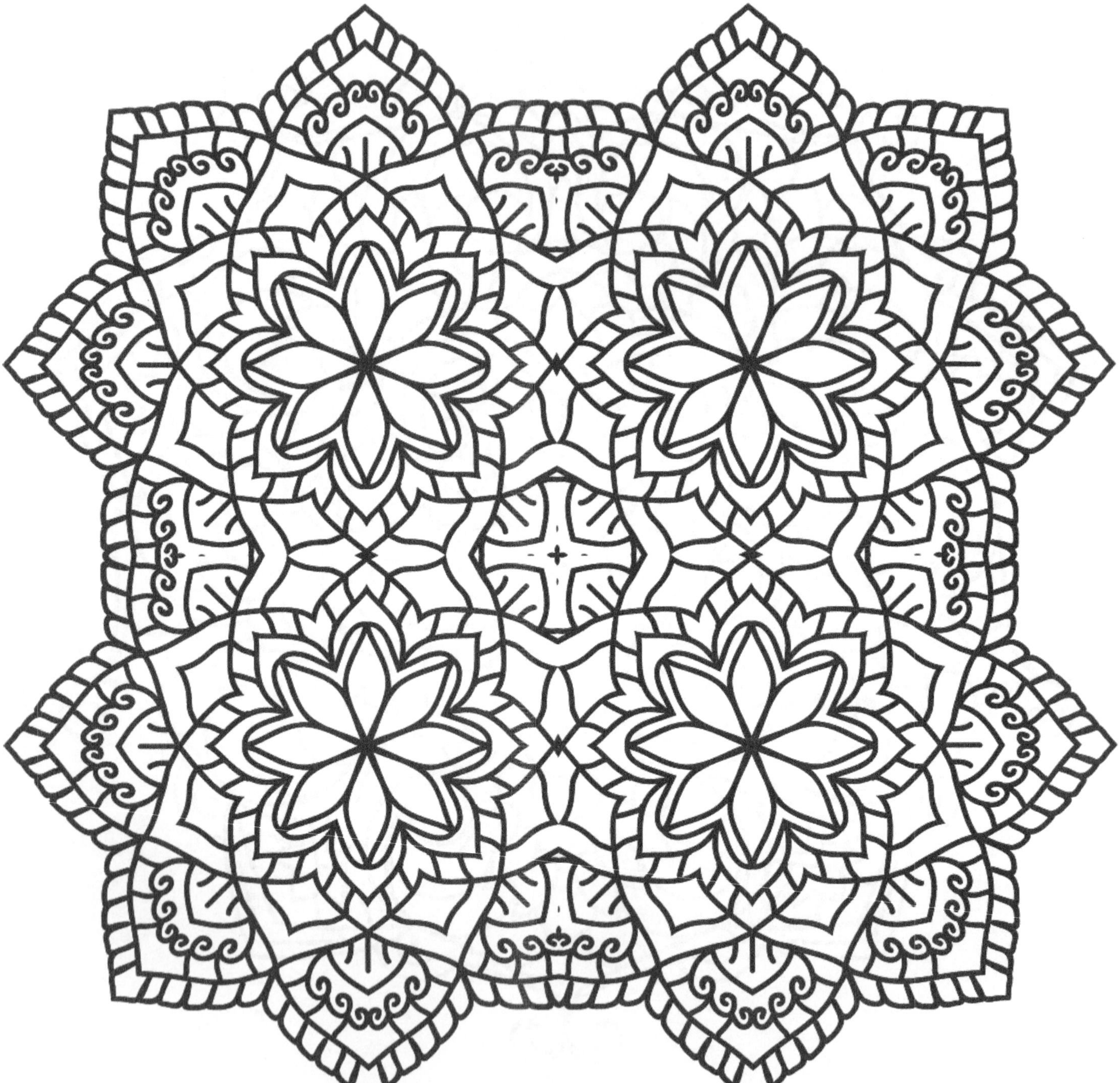

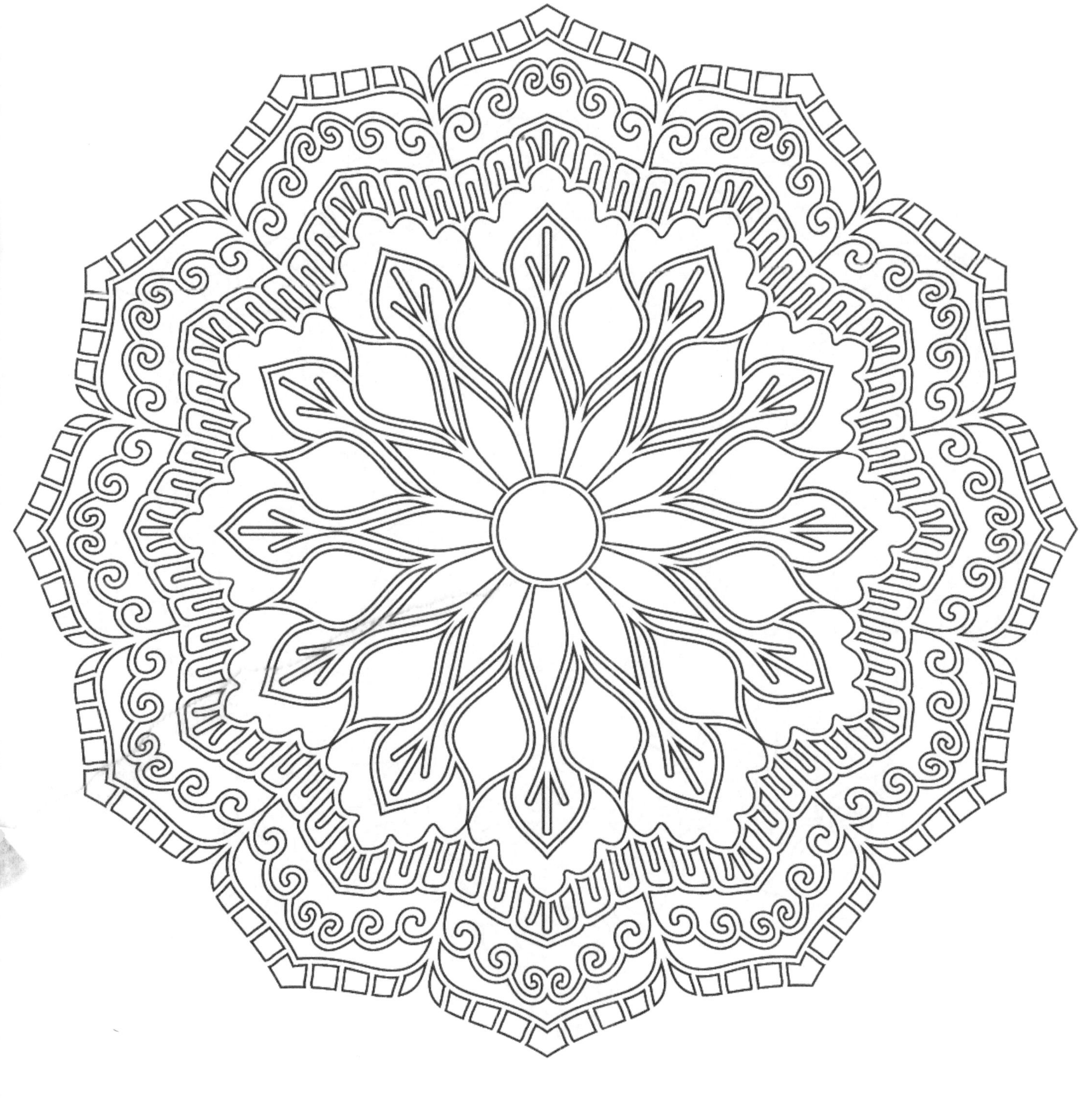

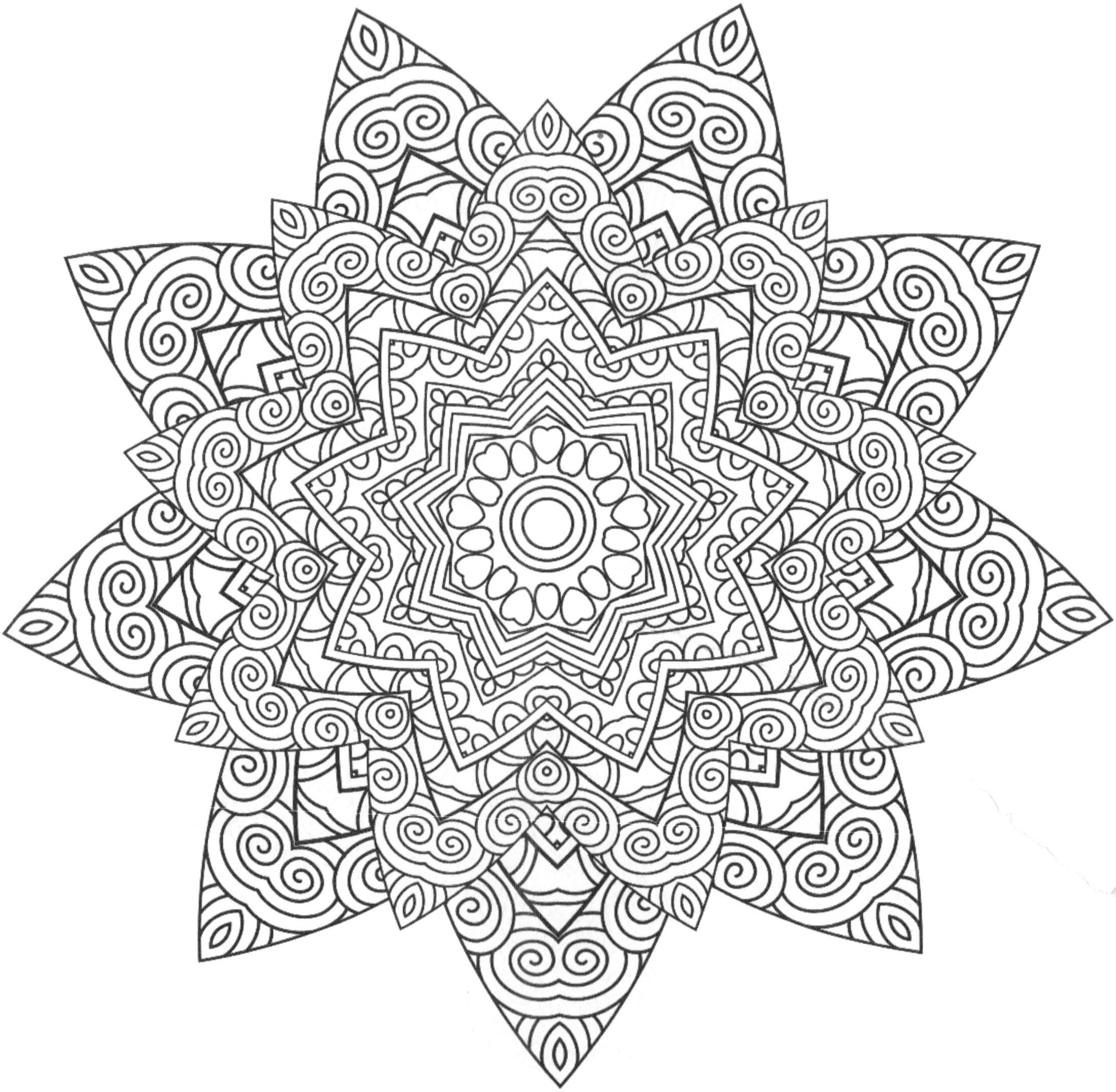

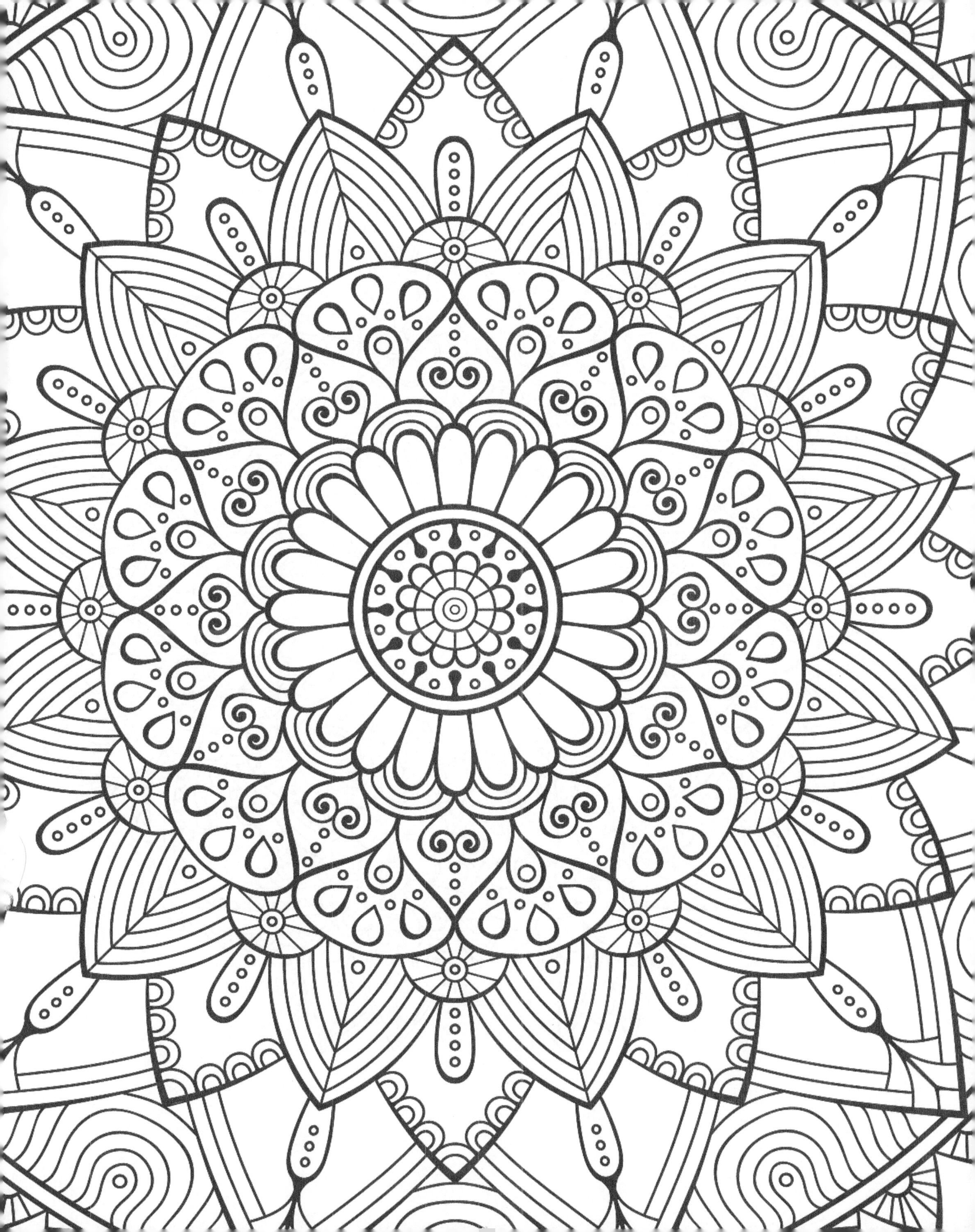

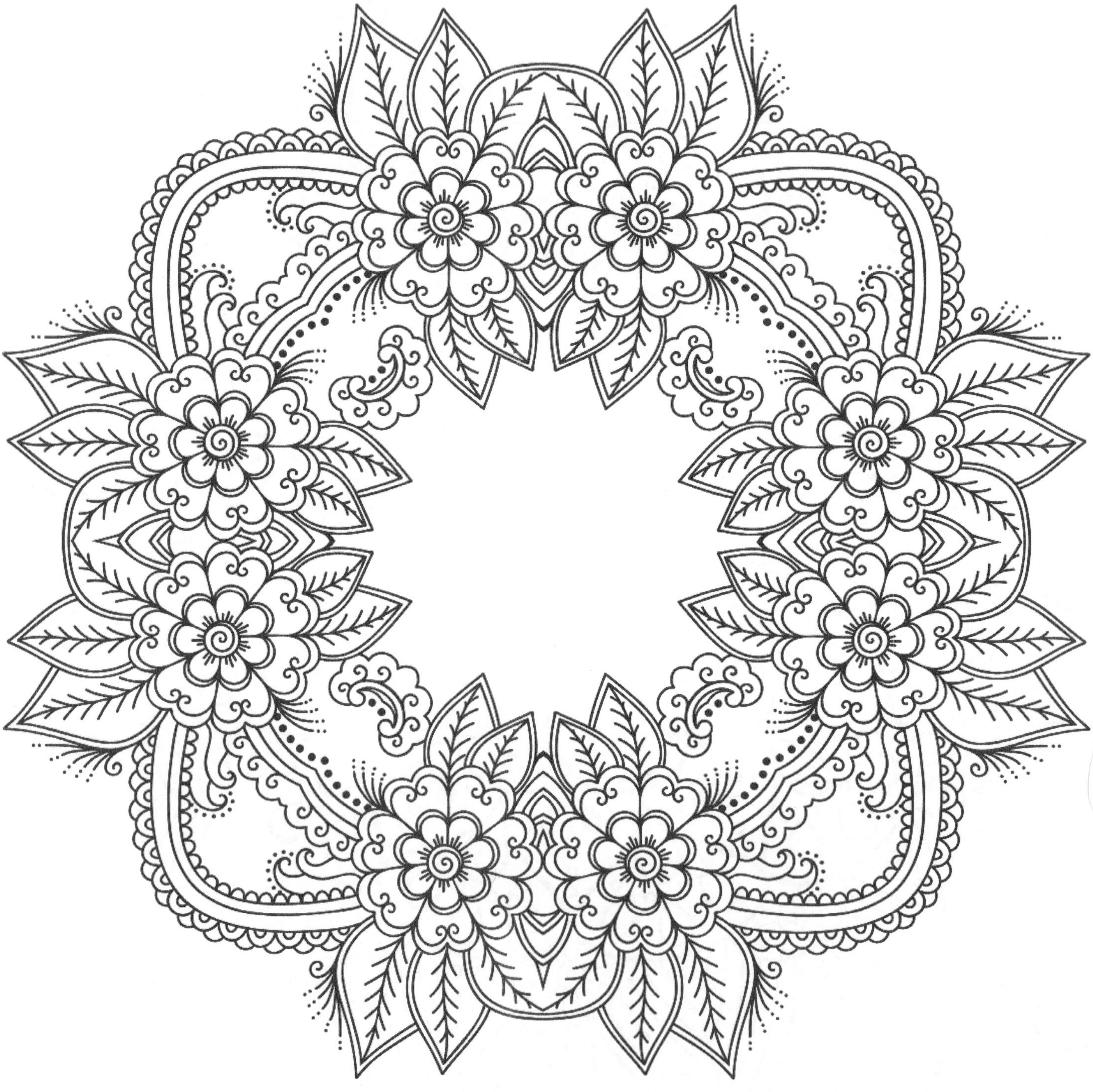

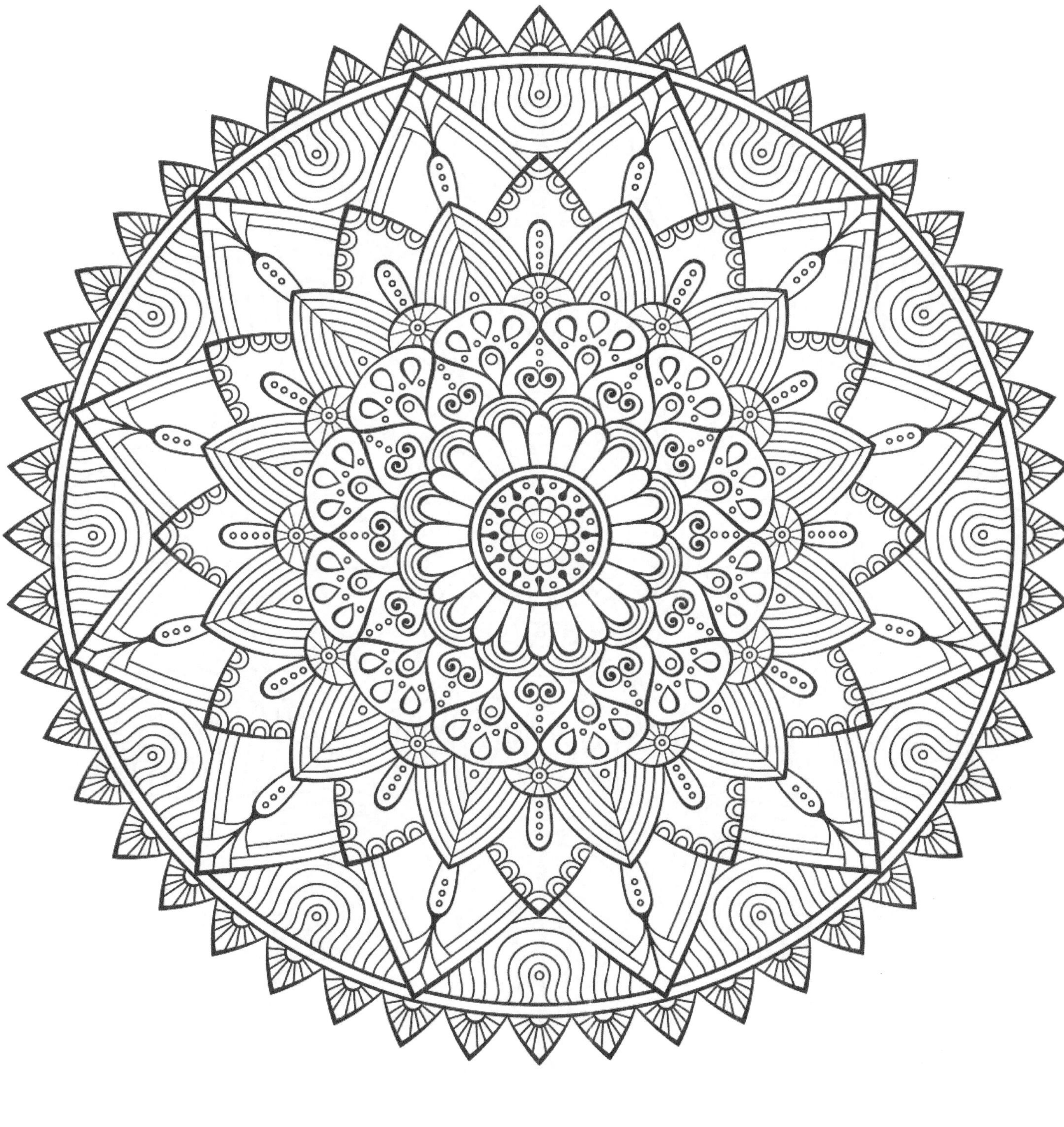

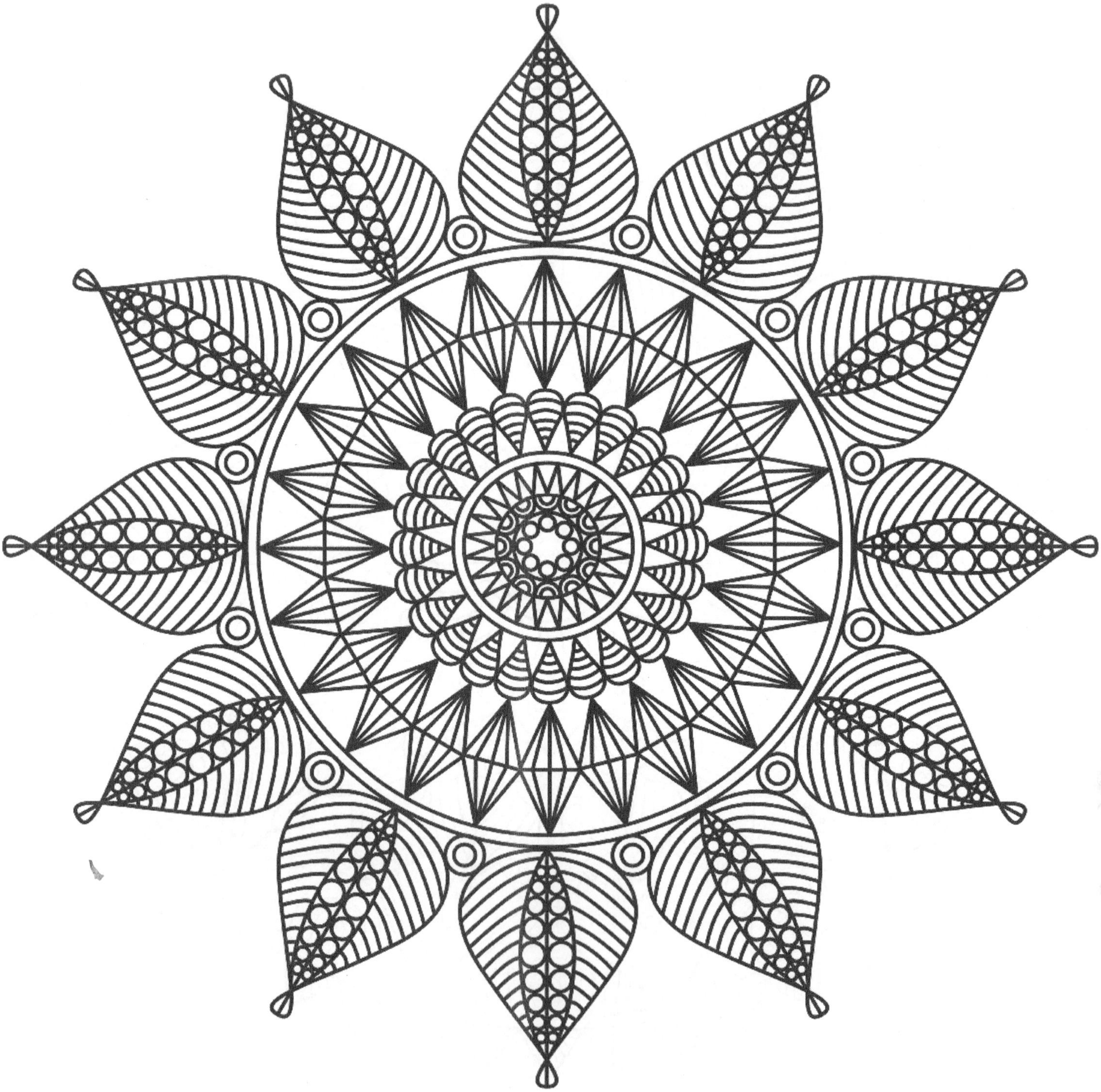

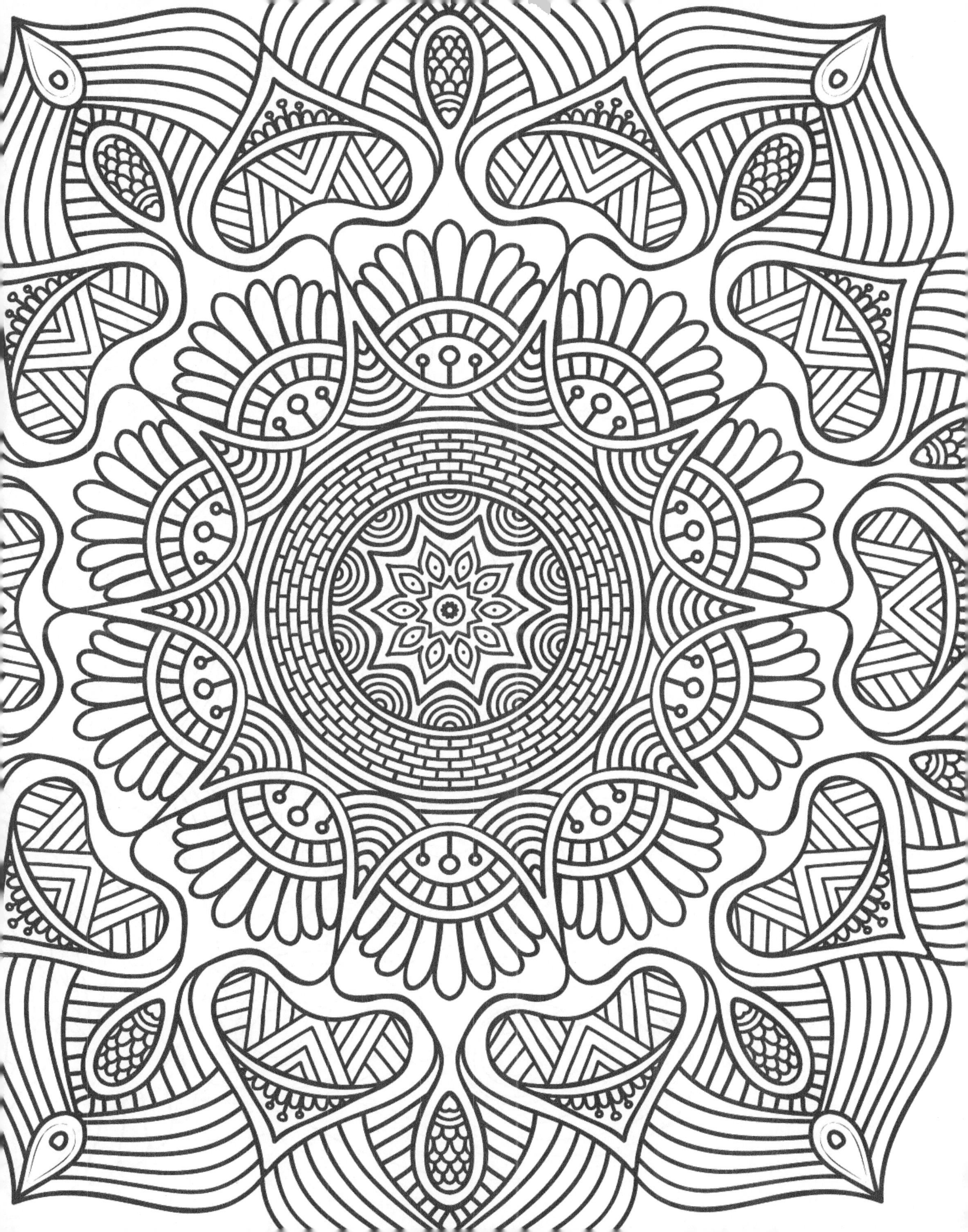

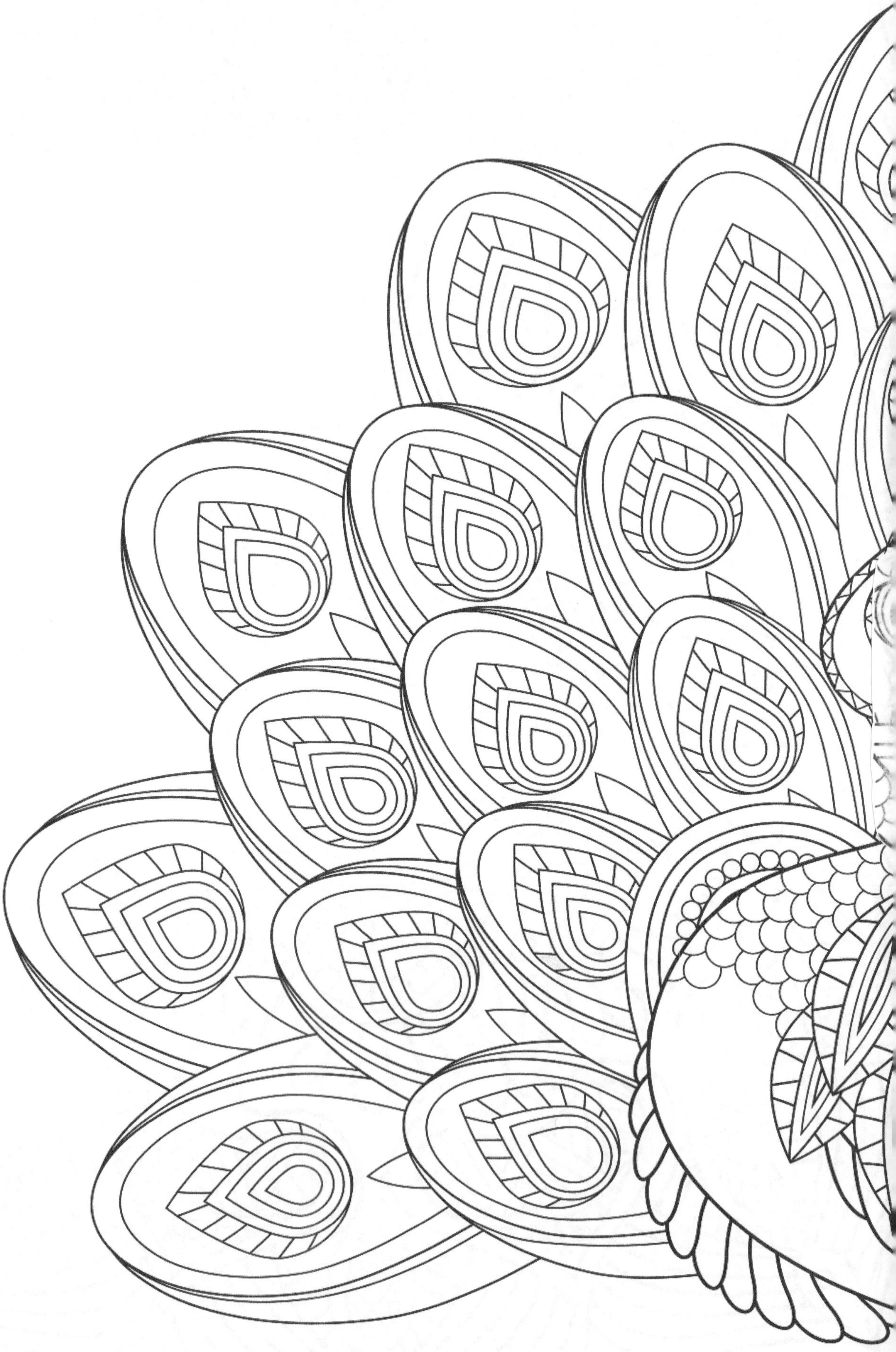

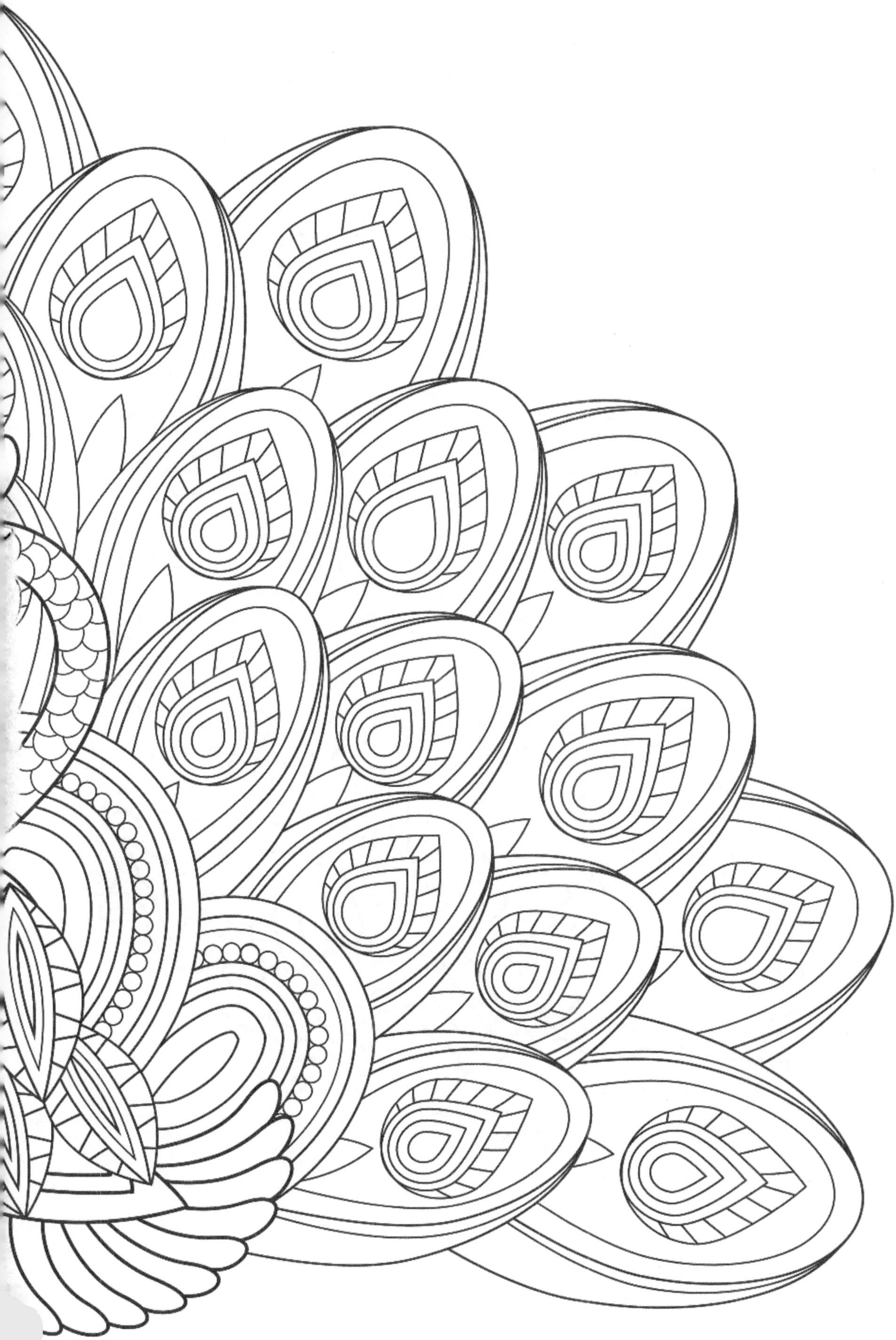

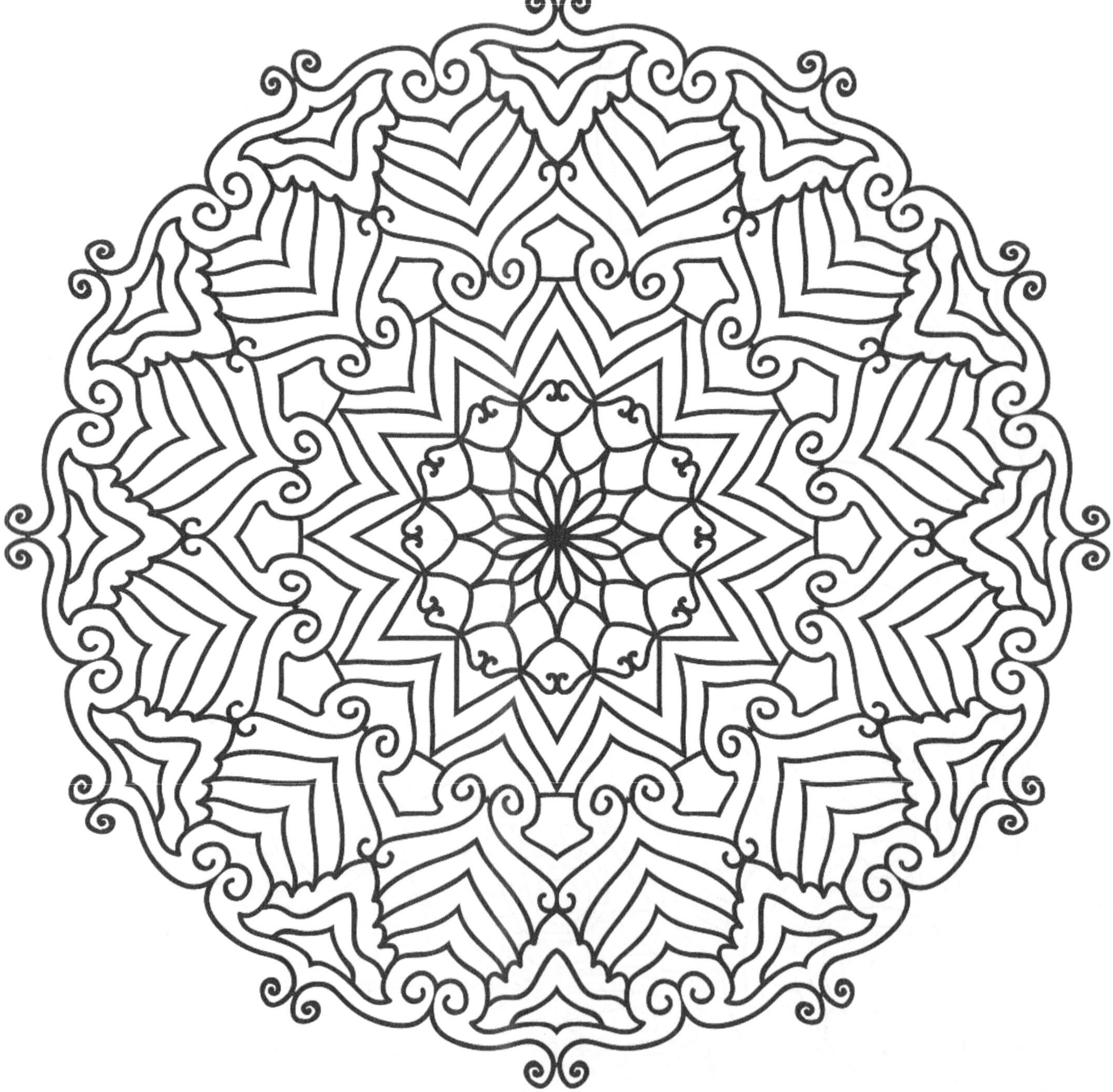

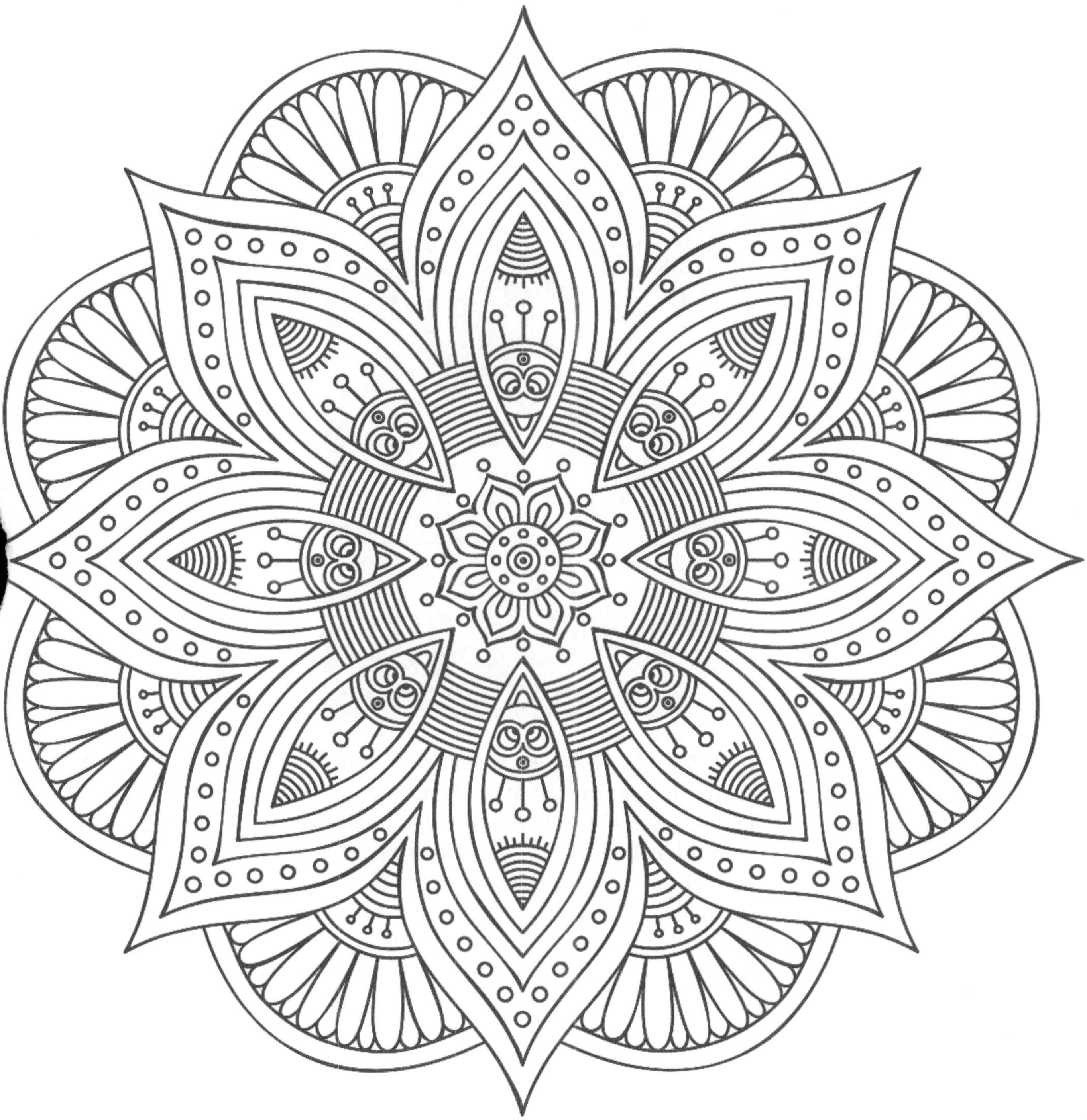

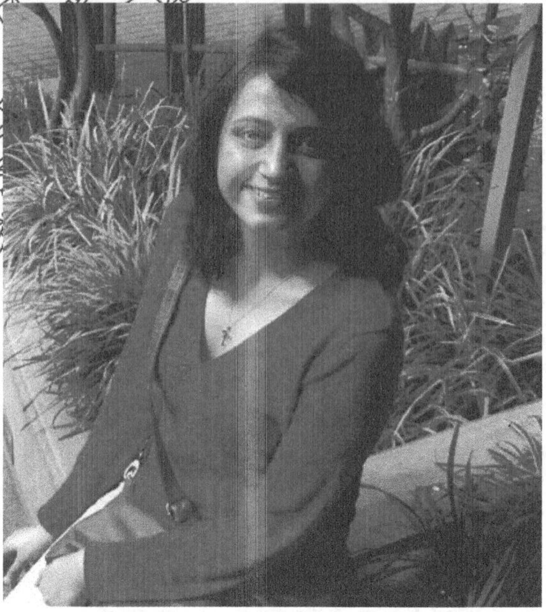

BHAVI MEHTA is a freelance designer currently working out of her home studio in Pune. A graduate of the National Institute of Fashion Technology, New Delhi, she specializes in print design, books in particular. After graduating, she worked with Penguin Books India from 2008 to 2013.